The Nicl

501 ideas for creating a
happy, productive workplace

1.   Introduction

Ideas for creating joy at work

> "Happiness and contentment at work is not about sushi for lunch and massages at your desk, it is about how bosses treat those that work for them."
>
> Professor Cary Cooper

At Happy we seek to create joy at work, for ourselves and for our clients. Generally we see this as about creating a culture based on trust and freedom, and creating environments where people enjoy coming to work and can feel fulfilled. As I set out in the introduction to The Happy Manifesto:

"Imagine a workplace where people are energised and motivated by being in control of the work they do. Imagine they are trusted and given freedom, within clear guidelines, to decide how to achieve their results. Imagine they are able to get the life balance they want. Imagine they are valued according to the work they do, rather than the number of hours they spend at their desk."

The Happy Manifesto laid down a set of principles and ideas for how to create happy, productive workplaces. What I've found since the Manifesto's publication is that people love the ideas and really value practical steps that companies have taken – "nickables" that you can put into practice in your organisation. This playbook is packed with such ideas.

Interspersed are case studies of organisations that follow these trust-based principles.

Some of the ideas here are from organisations that have specifically sought to apply the ideas in the Happy Manifesto, some are from Happy and some are taken from books and magazines. Feel free to nick them.

This is a work in progress. If you have examples from your own experience, please do send them to me at henry@happy.co.uk.

Enjoy!

Contents

2. Trust your people

Our experience is that people work best when they are trusted and given freedom, within guidelines, to use their own judgement. How do you, as a manager, step out of approval and instead "pre-approve" and focus on supporting your people?

Trust based workplaces

Research shows that what works is empowering people: Dr. Kamal Birdi of the University of Sheffield and six other researchers studied the productivity of 308 companies across twenty-two years. They found that approaches like "total quality management" and "just-in-time inventory control" had no consistent effect on productivity.

This research is quoted by Lazslo Bock (Head of People at Google) in his book Work Rules: "So what did? Performance improved only when companies implemented programs to empower employees (for example, by taking decision-making authority away from managers and giving it to individuals or teams), provided learning opportunities that were outside what people needed to do their jobs, increased their reliance on teamwork (by giving teams more autonomy and allowing them to self-organize), or a combination of these."

Customer service is about trust. "The secret behind great customer service: trust your employees to serve the customers the way they want to", explained Timpsons founder John Timpson

Timpsons has two rules: Dress the part and put the money in the till. After that it is up to each branch to decide how to operate.

Get rid of the Quality Improvement Team: Ulysses Lyons, Principal at Nuneaton Sixth Form College, explained how, they had moved to "doing with" rather than "doing to", having full stakeholder engagement in innovation – rather than a separate team that takes responsibility for quality: "Doing away with the quality improvement team is the best way to improve quality."

Set up systems to make it inevitable that people do the right thing: "Stop putting blocks in people's way, instead make it easy, inevitable that they do what's right. Allow people to be people." Donna Reeves

Nelson's empowered navy: General Stanley McChrystal describes (in Team of Teams) how, in the 1800s, the French and Spanish navies were based on orders from a central command. "by tradition, commanders of individual ships awaited orders transmitted in flag signals".

In contrast, "Nelson crafted an organizational culture that rewarded individual initiative and critical thinking, as opposed to simple execution of commands." At the Battle of Trafalgar he sent his ships to disrupt the enemy lines, knowing his commanders would be able to act on the spot, while the other side waited for orders. Britain lost none of its 27 ships but destroyed 19 of the enemies' 33 ships.

No approval needed at Netflix: In "Rules, No Rules", Jennifer Nierva describes how at her previous job, at Hewlett-Packard, she had to get 20 levels of approval to employ consultants on a $200,000 contract. It took her six weeks and endless frustrating phone calls.

Joining Netflix she came up with a $1 million marketing proposal and asked her boss who she had to get to sign it off. "Nobody", was the answer. "Just sign it and send it back."

"At most companies, the boss is there to approve or block the decisions of employees. This is a surefire way to limit innovation and slow down growth. When the boss steps out of the role of

A $700 million power plant from self-management and trust: In Reinventing Organisations, Frederick Laloux gives the example of newly hired Shazad Qasim at power company AES. He wanted to return to Pakistan and research the potential for AES to provide electricity generation there. CEO Dennis Bakke was very doubtful and wouldn't have himself approved it but, under AES self-managing rules, the decision was Shazad's. He went back to Pakistan, created a new position for himself and, two-and-a-half years later, AES had a $700 million power plant built and creating electricity there.

No scripts, trust your people: For Zappos, the online shoe retailer bought by Amazon for a billion dollars, the focus is on trust: "When customers call us, instead of giving our employees scripts to read, we believe that trusting our employees and giving them the freedom to do whatever it takes to make our customers happy ultimately will result in happier customers," said Tony Hsieh, CEO of Zappos.

Check it's above the waterline: At WL Gore there is a concept of above the waterline and below the waterline. "Everyone at Gore consults with other knowledgeable Associates before taking actions that might be 'below the waterline,' causing serious damage to the enterprise" (From Brave New Work).

Freedom at Facebook: "At any given point in time, there isn't just one version of Facebook running, there are probably 10,000.", explained Marc Zuckerberg in this podcast. "Any engineer at the company can basically decide that they want to test something. There are some rules on sensitive things, but in general, an engineer can test something, and they can launch a version of

11

Facebook not to the whole community, but maybe to 10,000 people or 50,000 people—whatever is necessary to get a good test of an experience."

"And then, they get a readout of how that affected all of the different metrics, and things that we care about. How were people connecting? How were people sharing? Do people have more friends in this version? Of course, business metrics, like how does this cost the efficiency of running the service, how much revenue are we making?" (https://bit.ly/EntZuck)

Pre approval

It is common to ask people to solve a problem, or come up with an improvement to a service, and bring it back for approval. The concept of pre-approval is that you miss out that last step. As the manager you approve the solution before your people have come up with a solution. Instead you agree clear guidelines (budget, requirements, metrics, who they should talk to) and leave them to implement a solution.

Pre approval for the new web site at TLC: "One of our other key elements over the last couple of years has been freedom within clear guidelines. We very much use pre-approval. We did some work at the beginning about working out what the brand guidelines were and what being Brand Guardian meant, and then we've said, 'off you go, it's up to you, you're our marketing expert'.

"Some of the differences that we've seen in how we've built a brand are just amazing. Our new website launched about six weeks ago. The first day I saw the website was the day after it launched. The first few weeks Paige was asking me, 'what do you think about this colour, what do you think about this font', but I reminded her to go back to what we said about pre-approval. She knew the outcome we were aiming to get for. You almost saw her

come to life, because actually she's really creative, she thinks really quickly, she wants to test new things, and actually the website is amazing. The difference that we've seen in traffic through to the website in the last month is unbelievable."
Michelle Hill, CEO, TLC

(2017 Happy Workplaces CEO conference, https://happymanifesto.com/2018/07/11/pre-approval-in-practice-at-tlc/)

Get your most junior staff to make the key decisions: GCHQ, one of the UK's intelligence agencies, needs to be at the forefront of technology. So a group of staff secured a £1 million budget from directors for innovation. They set up a crowdsourcing site, OneShot, where staff could post a request. It might be £500 for this idea or £8,000 for that piece of technology.

In most companies, the decision on who got the money would be made by senior managers or directors. At GCHQ they split the £1 million into 100 sets of £10,000 and gave that amount to the most junior members of staff to decide.

One person explained how they had an idea for a piece of technology that would vastly improve communications, but would cost £10,000. Previously it might have required 5 levels of approval and they probably wouldn't have bothered. But they put it up on OneShot, it was fully funded within a week and implemented within two weeks. The effect was to hugely increase the speed of decision-making, but also to change who made the decisions, to people closer to the front line.

$2,000 without approval to please a guest: At Ritz Carlton employees can spend up to $2,000 to satisfy a guest or deal with any issues (McCrystal)

Give your staff power, and £500, to resolve issues. At Timpsons staff are expected to use their judgement in dealing with any problems and can spend up to £500 to settle a complaint. "It has saved us a fortune" explained founder John Timpson

SocialAdventures: staff can spend £250 without checking: Chief Executive Scott Darrugh describes how managers got frustrated with having to approve minor spending, and with basic maintenance not getting done. So they said anybody could spend up to £250 on anything they felt was needed.

"Not only did it free up management time, and make sure problems got fixed quickly", explains Scott, "but it also led to a 6% fall in spending."

Improving your people's work takes away the ownership: A director at the UK's National Audit Office explained when he got it about "improving" work: "A decade ago I took a report from my team and spent two days transforming it. When I gave it back, the team manager came to me and said. 'What you have produced is undoubtedly a better report. However you have completely taken away the ownership from my team and demotivated them.' It made me realise I had to find a different way to get that result."

Set high expectations but don't check the detail: "When I was at McKinsey & Company, I had a manager named Andrew who expected perfection in the market analyses I prepared for clients. But he didn't micromanage me by telling me how to write each page or how to do my analyses. Andrew set our expectations higher. In 1999 we were serving a financial services company and doing one of the first e-commerce projects our firm had ever done.

"I brought a draft report to him and instead of editing it, he asked, "Do I need to review this?" I knew deep down that while my report was good, he would surely find some room for improvement. Realizing this, I told him it wasn't ready and went back to refine it further. I came back to him a second time, and a second time he asked, "Do I need to review this?" I went away again. On my fourth try, he asked the same question and I told him, "No. You don't need to review it. It's ready for the client." He answered, "Terrific. Nice work." And sent it to the client without even glancing at it."

Laszlo Bock, Head of People, Google in Work Rules

Spend what's needed at Netflix: Reed Hastings describes in "No Rules" an incident where they were set to demonstrate House of Cards on the latest Samsung TV, to the Washington Post tech journalist. Nigel Baptiste, Director of Partner Engagement, arrived to find the TV had been disposed of with other TVs they'd asked facilities to get rid of. He tried calling suppliers and none had that TV.

Then Nick, the most junior engineer on our team, sprinted into the office. "Don't worry, Nigel," Nick said. "I solved that. I came in last night, and I saw the TV had been disposed of. You didn't respond to my calls and texts. So I drove out to the Best Buy in Tracy, bought the same TV, and tested it this morning. It cost twenty-five hundred dollars, but I thought it was the right thing to do."

As Reed points out Nick had used five words to guide his actions: "Act in Netflix's best interests"

Don't check with the boss: John, explains: "When I started at Happy, I would email Henry - the founder - with every bit of expenditure. He soon wrote back: 'John, if it's under £400 and you think we need it, buy it. If it's over £400, check with someone, but no need to check with me.'"

The Advice Process

> "Make sure that all members of the organization can make any decision, as long as they consult with the people affected and the people who have expertise on the matter."

The Advice Process is based on individuals taking responsibility, rather than seeking consensus. Corporate Rebels explains it like this:

- Someone notices a problem or opportunity and takes the initiative, or alerts someone better placed to do so.

- Prior to a proposal, the decision-maker may seek input to gather perspectives before proposing action.

- The initiator makes a proposal and seeks advice from those affected or those with expertise.

- Taking this advice into account, the decision-maker decides on an action and informs those who have given advice. (From)

Usually, the decision maker is the person whose area is most affected, or who initiated an idea, or discovered a problem, or saw an opportunity.

Changing prices at Happy: Two colleagues, John and Ben, decided our pricing was out of date. They analysed the market, found out what competitors were charging, and consulted colleagues. But the decision was made neither by consensus nor consent. After seeking advice, John and Ben decided on the new pricing model. It represented substantial increases. (I told them I didn't agree. However, it was not my decision to make.) The new pricing was put in place.

I have to admit I was probably wrong. Thirty-four years after founding Happy, I was too wedded to our old models. Indeed, without that increase, and its impact on our bank balance, we might not have survived the pandemic.

As a manager, make few or no decisions

The traditional approach is for the manager or leader to be seen as the expert, able to make the best decisions. The alternative is to coach your people, who are closer to where the decision will be implemented, to find their own solution. The role of the manager is no longer to show how clever you are, but instead to show how clever your people are.

> "Your job as a leader is not to be the smartest person in the room. It is to maximise the potential of your team." Liz Wiseman

Commit to making no decisions, but with an exception: When David Marquet was made Commander of the Sante Fe submarine, he realised he had been trained for a different model and didn't know how this one worked. That was the impetus for him deciding to make no decisions, but to instead coach his staff to make all decisions. There was one exception: If missiles were to be launched, that would still fall to him.

This was based on ensuring there was Competence and Clarity of Intent. The result was that the Sante Fe moved from being underperforming to being the best performing submarine in US Navy history. "And all this with a Captain who was a dummy and made no decisions", commented David Marquet in his excellent animated video.

Get the boss to make no decisions: "At B&Q we got two store managers to agree to make no decisions for three months. Instead they would coach their staff to decide for themselves. Over that period every KPI improved in those stores, and staff could respond immediately to customers.

As one said 'The shackles have been removed. We can now say to a customer 'yes I can do that for you.'" Donna Reeves

Be the boss just one day a week: When Alison Kriel was headteacher of Northwold Primary School in Hackney she only acted as headteacher one day in six. Each member of her management team (the deputies and the key stage heads) took on the role of head of the school for a day in a rota. "It certainly made succession planning easier", Alison commented

Get out of the way and watch performance increase: Inspired by the Marquet and B&Q examples I resolved to aim to make as few decisions as possible as the boss at Happy. For each of the next two years (before the pandemic hit) sales rose by over 25% and we moved from a loss to a significant profit.

Avoid Decisions: "We are seeking to avoid top level decisions. Take the staff conference: The team organised this themselves, I just turned up on the day. It was within budget and a fabulous day." Katherine Horler, Chief Executive, Adviza

No decisions for CEO: Kevin Rogers, Chief Executive of Paycare (a health cash plan provider in Wolverhampton) took up the Happy challenge of making no decisions for a quarter, from Jan 2019. "It was our best quarter in more than ten years. I decided to continue doing it and ask the next level of Directors to try it too."

No budgets: "At Mayden we work without expenditure budgets. For twenty years we have worked on basis people spend what is needed." Chris May, founder, Mayden

> "I rarely attend meetings and almost never make decisions We recently had a cocktail party to celebrate the 10-year anniversary since I last made a decision"
>
> Ricardo Semler, CEO Semco (Maverick)

Let staff decide their own expenses: In his excellent book "Becoming a Better Boss", Julian Birkinshaw describes a very interesting experiment at the pharma multi-national Roche. Two groups of staff, in Germany and Switzerland, were told that their travel claims were to become self-authorised.

Instead of being approved in advance and signed off afterwards, each employee would decide for themselves what was needed (though still aware of company policy). Instead of being checked, the resulting expenses would be displayed on the intranet. Julian describes the results as "astonishing": 45% of participants said their motivation had increased from being trusted in this way (against 6% feeling uncomfortable with the approach), and 3 in 4 said it was more efficient and took less time.

Salesforce executive Vala Afshar, Chief Digital Evangelist at Salesforce, tweeted "You likely have to get management approval for a $500 expense ... but you can call a 1 hour meeting with 20 people and no one notices."

Involve Your People

Vote on key decisions: The 55,000 strong healthcare company Davita puts democracy into practice by having staff vote on important decisions. Traci Fenton, CEO, WorldBlu

Let them work it out: "One manager runs a programme in three towns that needs 12 participants in order to be viable. He had told the staff this several times and each time it ran there were less than 12 young people on it. After hearing you speak he took along all the financial information and let the team work out for themselves what was needed for the programme to go ahead and cover its costs.

"The answer was 12 participants! But there was a different result, because the staff had reached that conclusion. Each programme now has more than 12 young people on it, the young people are benefiting, and we have a happy commissioner who will continue to buy the programme!

Katherine Horler, Chief Executive, Adviza

Think like business innovators: Gary Hamel, in Humanocracy, described a "mid Western US manufacturing company" where "over the course of a year, more than thirty thousand employees, many of them blue-collar union members, were taught how to think like business innovators. Out of this effort came thousands of game-changing ideas.

In one memorable, though not unusual, case, a long-tenured assembly line worker hatched an idea that ultimately produced a multimillion-dollar payoff. For the first time in her career, this woman had been asked to think big, and when the chance came, she grabbed it."

Trade unions are your friends

SouthWest Airlines, profitable every year for 40 years, is 82% unionised: Founder Herb Kelleher's people-based philosophy extended to treating the unions as partners. A US trade union web site notes that SouthWest has "the best relationship with its unions, and the highest customer satisfaction ratings". In 2008 the Transport Workers Union made Herb an honorary lifetime member" in grateful appreciation for [his] unparalleled Leadership in creating a magnificent airline and a generation of Employees who love coming to work."

Rotas

Let teams set the shift pattern: Advanced Technology Services (ATS) maintains equipment in other company's factories. Seeking to reduce time out of action, Site Manager Damien O'Neill consulted the customer, thought hard about the business implications and discussed with the team before coming up with the best and fairest solution he could think of to change the working pattern for his team and improve the service.

The new shift pattern did not go down well. Within a few days several of his team told him they may have to leave. He started to hear rumours of arguments at home over the impact of the new shift patterns. Despite his best efforts the team were not happy.

Damien stepped back, he remembered what he had learnt about involving teams and handing over power to them for the biggest decisions that affected them. He took a bold move. He called the team together, admitted he had got it wrong and asked them to come up with their own solution.

The team went away and came back with a completely new shift pattern where each person only worked a four-day week but where the equipment could be serviced 18 hours a day every day in line with the running of the factory. This new solution saved the client £11,000 per year.

And, crucially, the team completely bought into their own solution, they were happy with it, and motivated to make it work. The Union agreed the changes instantly since it had been suggested by its members.

Get your people to design the rotas: At United Utilities (a water and sewerage company in the North-West of England) the customer Services Director wanted to change the call centre from 9 to 5 weekday working to around-the-clock. She asked the front-line staff to design the new work patterns:

"The people, my people, designed the work patterns. I have working grandparents work patterns, I have 'I go out every Friday night and get absolutely trollied so don't ask me to work a Friday night but I will work any other night that you want me to work' work patterns. I am a heavily trade unionised business. I have nearly 80% Trade Union representation. It went straight through. Why? Because the employees had designed the work patterns.

They weren't just new work patterns, they were extended opening hours."

Louise Beardmore, Customer Services Director, United Utilities, 2017 Happy Workplace conference

Setting salaries in a trust-based workplace

Let your people choose the CEO salary: At Happy we, as of 2021, let the staff decide the salary of the head of the company (actually our Chief Happiness Officer). He presents his case, and how much he is requesting, and the employees fill in a one question survey to state the rise they propose.

In the first year Henry proposed a rise of 4.2%, on top of inflation. Overall the response was an offer of 5%, with one person saying "I'd double that" and another proposing three times. "I felt very valued by the responses", said Henry.

Train your people in financials and then let them set their own salaries: Pim de Morree, of Corporate Rebels described a Dutch IT company, who employ about 300 people. The first step they did was opening up the salary levels to everyone in the company to show it was fair and if it was not fair, in the opinion of the employees, they had to think of a solution.

So first they train them in the basic financials and then they involved them in setting their own salaries to become more entrepreneurs than just simply employees. Most people did not raise their salaries higher than the normal pay raises and they actually set their salary increases lower than management would normally have. They would do this in teams.

Set your own salaries with peer advice: Another Dutch company, in financial consultancy, encourages staff to set their own salary, then ask advice from their team members whether that's too high or too low and they use that advice to come up with their final decision. So the individual decides in the end but they listen to the advice of their peers. And the peer pressure, or the peer control, whatever you want to call it, actually does it's work there. (Corporate Rebels)

Decide salaries at a panel: At Happy we have a salary panel of four and all are elected by our staff. The employees also decide the size of the salary pot, based on current finances. Then people put their case for an increase and the panel decides.

Let staff decide the approach: "We have set up a working group of staff to evaluate what enables somebody to progress and what the salary policy should be." Katharine Horler, CEO, Adviza

Let The Money Gang decide: At Brighton-based Nixon McInnes a committee made up of board members and those elected by staff approves all salary decisions. Employees submit their own proposals and the "Money Gang" decides if it is fair and affordable. (Worldblu, 50 transformational practices)

3.   Case Study: Buurtzorg

Imagine a company with 15,000 staff and no managers. Imagine annual sales of over 300 million euros and no Chief Financial Officer, with only six people working in finance. Imagine it has grown to that size from, 11 years ago, having just four staff – although it is not-for-profit and has no venture capital investment.

The organisation is Buurtzorg which, in those 11 years, has gone from providing 0% of Dutch community nursing care to over two thirds. Without those layers of management it is uniquely focused on the front-line staff, the nurses, and on the needs of the patients.

"We have not had one management meeting since we started", explains Jos. "In my former job we had a lot of meetings that were only about meetings. Now we just have time to solve the problems."

The Buurtzorg model is based on traditional Dutch care, with nurses based in local communities. In the 80s and 90s this approach was changed to introduce the "efficiency" of modern management methods. Centralised call centres took the calls from patients and central planners would be allocated the jobs to nurses, and the time to spend with each person. A patient might see dozens of different nurses over a year, and have to explain their problems anew to each one.

Buurtzorg has returned to a nurse-led approach. There are no call centres. Nurses take the calls. Where elsewhere head-office planners decide who visits who, nurses - in self-managing teams of ten to twelve nurses - plan patient visits and decide how long they spend there, depending on their judgement of the need.

With only 45 people in the head office, overhead costs are 8% instead of the 25% that is standard in the industry.

"When nurses feel happy … they will do good things"

With nurses able to fulfil their vocation and respond according to their judgement, staff satisfaction is high and sickness among staff is a little over half that of other care companies. And Buurtzorg is consistently top for patient satisfaction, out of over 300 Dutch nursing providers.

For Jos de Blok, there are three simple principles behind the success:

1. Do what's needed
2. Reflect on what you are doing, and try to do it better
3. Use your common sense (or "common sensing" as Jos puts it)

"Let's avoid complexity. Even with 14,000 people, it can be a very simple organisation. We must build organisations based on meaningful relationships. When nurses feel happy they will stay healthy and they will do good things."

As important as the self-managing teams it's the total focus on the patient need.

A group of nurses within the organization had noticed that when their elderly patients suffered a fall, they often broke their hips, which reduced their autonomy (sometimes permanently). So they created a new program focused on accident prevention and delivered it in their local market. They were so excited with the results that they brought them to Buurtzorg CEO Jos de Blok.

This program should be rolled out across the entire company, they said. But instead of assigning a task force or piloting the program in other regions or announcing it as a company-wide initiative, he did something else entirely. He asked the team to write a story about what they'd created and publish it to the company's internal social network, along with a guidebook for how to stand up the program. If the idea was good, he reasoned, it would spread.

More care for the client takes less time: "A 2009 Ernst & Young study found that Buurtzorg requires, on average, close to 40 percent fewer hours of care per client than other nursing organizations—which is ironic when you consider that nurses in Buurtzorg take time for coffee and talk with the patients, their families, and neighbours, while other nursing organizations have come to time "products" in minutes.", Frederick Laloux (Laloux, Reinventing organisations")

Why? "Patients stay in care only half as long, heal faster, and become more autonomous."

Huge savings to the Dutch health care system: "A third of emergency hospital admissions are avoided, and when a patient does need to be admitted to the hospital, the average stay is shorter. The savings for the Dutch social security system are considerable—Ernst & Young estimates that close to €2 billion would be saved in the Netherlands every year if all home care organizations achieved Buurtzorg's results." (Laloux, Reinventing organisations)

4. Make your people feel good

Nearly everybody we have asked agrees with the statement "people work best when they feel good about themselves". If that is true, it makes sense to make that (creating an environment where people feel good about themselves) a focus of leadership and management. Here's some ideas on how to do it:

> "Employees in the new workforce aren't looking for amenities such as game rooms, free food and fancy latte machines. But they are looking for benefits and perks that will improve their wellbeing — those that offer them greater flexibility, autonomy and the ability to lead a better life." Jim Clifton, Jim Harper, Gallup (It's the Manager)

Start each meeting with a positive: That is item zero at every meeting at Lego ("a Danish company you might have heard of"), explained Alex Kjerulf (Chief Happiness Officer, WooHoo) at a Happy Workplaces conference. Participants split into pairs and share something that has gone well. The result is more co-operation and shorter meetings.

The benefit of engaged staff: "When Gallup analyzed the differences in performance between engaged and actively disengaged business/work units, work units scoring in the top quartile on employee engagement significantly outperformed those in the bottom quartile on these crucial performance outcomes:

41% lower absenteeism 24% less turnover (in high-turnover organizations) 59% less turnover (in low-turnover organizations) 28% less shrinkage 70% fewer safety incidents 58% fewer patient safety incidents 40% fewer defects (quality) 10% higher customer ratings 17% higher productivity 20% higher sales, 21% higher profitability" Jim Clifton, Jim Harper, Gallup (It's the Manager)

Build relationships

"We got lots of advice on how to scale the business but none on how to scale our relationships. Good relationships at work make you feel trusted, respected, understood, empowers, supported, appreciated, energised", Rosie Brown, MD, Cook

Take time to talk: "Every day, take five minutes to talk to one of your employees with no other agenda. Just go up and ask how they are and what's going on." Alexander Kjerulf, Leading with Happiness

Take breaks together to improve productivity: MIT Professor Sandy Pentland studied interaction at a Bank of America call centre in 2008. When he shifted coffee breaks from individuals taking them on their own to being team based, interaction rose and call times (the key measure) dropped. When this break system was rolled out to all call centres, it result in $15 million saved in productivity. (McCrystal)

It's all about relationships: "Our sense of happiness and fulfilment across life depends on the quality of our relationships. Relationships drive business performance. We have 90 shops and the best performance comes from those with the best relationships". Rosie Brown, MD, Cook

Engage with your people: Take 5 minutes: each day speak to a different member of staff. Ask what can I do for you? Sarah Metcalfe, Happy Coffee Consulting

Ring 5 employees a week: "We have 230 staff. Now for half an hour on a Monday morning I ring 5 people I don't normally see. I love it and, from the emails I get afterwards, it seems they do too." Katherine Horler, Chief Executive, Adviza:

Lots of the best things are free: "Say thank you. Show appreciation. Care for others. Help everybody feel part of the community. These are all free." Sarah Gillard, Director, John Lewis Partnership

Create a culture of "I've got your back": Create a culture where everybody feels that others are absolutely on their side. Derek Hill, MD, ATS

Have Talking Partners: At NextJump everybody has a "talking partner", who they see several times a week and share their challenges and thoughts with. It is similar to a mentoring relationship but NextJump believes that conventional mentoring, where a senior person helps a junior member of staff, fails 95% of the time.

Talking partners is instead co-mentoring. "Start at the top, and partner with somebody different to you", suggests Tarun. "You push each other to go to the places you don't want to go." "The idea is that your partner's success is almost more important than your own", explained Henry Searle at Happy's 2016 Happy Workplace conference. Henry is co-Managing Director of the London office with Tarun and also his Talking Partner. At both conference speeches I have heard the Next Jump speaker came with their talking partner, whose role was totally supportive. Imagine having somebody in your organisation that is 100% there for you.

Doughnut buddies: Industrial maintenance company ATS uses the Donut feature in Slack. Every two weeks it randomly selects pairs, across the company, to meet for coffee (and, possibly, doughnuts). "It's become a real point of excitement", explained MD Derek Hill. "When it comes round, everybody is asking 'who is your buddy this time?'"

Written appreciation: "In the holiday period I write what I appreciate about each person on a star under the tree. They get to see and so do their colleagues." Annie McDowall, CEO, Share Community

Go for a walk: "Building relationships doesn't need to cost a fortune. We have ideas like 'Go and have a meeting walking on the South Downs'", Rosie Brown, MD, Cook

Get remote workers to meet: "We have lot of remote workers. So we have created clusters of four or five staff who live nearby and encourage them to meet up, after a day of interviewing clients, for coffee. For some it's once a month, for some it's every week." Katherine Horler, Chief Executive, Adviza

> "Three things in human life are important. The first is to be kind. The second is to be kind. And the third is to be kind." —Henry James

Joy at Work

Find purpose and passion: "Fear based leadership leads to command and control. Freedom based leadership leads to empowered workplaces. It's not about ping pong and perks. It's about purpose and passion." Derek Hill, MD, ATS

Help your people find joy at work: "Help them do something they are good at, working to their strengths and having the freedom to do it well. My goal is for all my team to get joy at work in 80% of what they do. I reckon I'm at 95%. Do what you love." Cathy Busani

Joy at work is the best route to quality: When the quality team at East London Foundation Trust checked what made teams work well and deliver quality provision, they found the key factor was having joy at work. As a result, they made the key quality focus one of creating joy at work.

"My role is to help teams feel they have permission to try different things.", explained Auzewell Chitewe. "It's not about what the organisation can do for them but about empowering the teams. In health care we have what we call wicked problems. You can't solve them doing things the way we always have. It's not about some geniuses figuring out a solution. It is about giving permission to those closest to the problem to come up with solutions, and specifically to involve the "service user" (or patient) in that solution. They have to have the freedom to fail."

> "In that moment, I realized why my other startups had failed and why Twitter was going to work. Twitter brought me joy. I was laughing out loud on a Sunday afternoon using the application that I had spent many days and nights working on. I was passionate about this project."
>
> Biz Stone, Things a little bird told me

Ask will it make us happier. When Ben Hunt-Davis and his team were training for the Sydney Olympics in 2000 (where they won Gold in rowing 8s) the key question at all times was "will it make the boat go faster?". (An extra hour training? Yes, it will make the boat go faster. A pint down the pub? No, so they didn't do it.)

"So we ask 'will it make us happier?' and 'will it make life better?' If the answer is No, we don't do it". Nikki Gatenby, CEO, Propellernet

Employee Passion: HCL decided to survey not just employee satisfaction (for which the company was ranked no. 1 in India in 2009) but also their passion, and to share the results. People got to think about what drove them to act passionately and how they could best leverage this at work.

Happiness as a Focus

> "The science is clear: Making other people happy makes you happier too." Arlette Bentzen, WooHoo

Make happiness the "ultimate purpose" of the business: That's what Spedan Lewis did in the 1920s when he set up the John

Lewis Partnership as a worker's mutual. Every decision was to be made on how happy it made the staff. With that core focus, the company has grown from 300 staff then to 85,000 now.

When I spoke on a panel alongside Charlie Mayfield, then Chair of the John Lewis Partnership, he explained that at the last Board meeting, five hours long, they spent just 20 minutes discussing the numbers. The rest was spent on how to motivate and develop our people."

Create a happiness plan: That's what the team of happiness ambassadors at Danish insurance company SEB does. Every year, just as you might have a sales plan, they create a plan of how to make SEB happier, explained Arlette Bentzen of WooHoo at the 2018 Happy Workplaces conference.

Seek arbejdsglaede: Only the Scandinavians have a word for work happiness, and this is it in Danish.

Happiness at work pays: When the Belgian Ministry of Social Security focused on happiness at work, results improved dramatically. Laurence Vanhee, Chief Happiness Officer, explained at the 2018 Happy Workplaces conference that productivity rose 20%, rental costs fell by 12 million euro, maintenance costs by 50%, spontaneous applications rose by 500%. Staff turnover fell by 75%.

Team Shout Out Board: "We have a board thanking your team for anything they have done for you. We share and shout them out in our Monday morning all team huddle meeting." Rosie Smith

Fun activities

Monthly home cooked lunch: "We have a monthly lunch where someone cooks at home and then brings it in to warm up and feed everyone at lunch. Different person cooks each month" Lawrence Parkin, Marketing Manager, Learning Nexus

Fun at work: NextJump is a company that believes in enjoying itself, from the summer outing to the annual dance battle. For the latter each office practices relentlessly for the big showdown. Remember that the core job is coding, people not known for their extrovertism, and flick through the video of the 2015 event: The new New York office is being built with a swimming pool on the roof, open all weekend with staff encouraged to bring their families.

Play music: "play music in toilets!, in reception spaces!, music makes a big difference" Katherine Billingham-Mohammed, Director, Sunshine Group Consulting

Liven up Fridays: "This was an idea from the Happy CEO breakfast. We set a budget of just £15 for people to do something different to liven up Fridays. One group brought in croissants and had a team breakfast, which they are now doing monthly. Another had a sunflower growing competition. One had a treasure hunt." Katherine Horler, Chief Executive, Adviza

> "People's happiness in their work is not about gourmet salads or sleeping pods or foosball tables. True and abiding happiness in work comes from being deeply engaged in solving a problem with talented people you know are also deeply engaged in solving it, and from knowing that the customer loves the product or service you all have worked so hard to make."
>
> Patty McCord, Chief Talent Officer, Netflix

Fulfilling Dreams

Help your people fulfil their dreams: Can you help your people fulfil their dreams at work? "One of our people was a mad keen cyclist so, when we got interest from Evans, he got to lead it. Another was committed to wildlife conservation in Africa. We teamed her up with a sustainable safari company in Namibia.

They pay us in safaris – it's very popular with staff!" Nikki Gatenby, CEO, Propellernet

Create a Dream Academy: "At Cook we have the Dream Academy to help our people achieve their personal dreams. Dream It. Plan it. Do It."

Since the COOK Dream Academy started in 2013, over 100 people – members of our team and customers – have had a series of confidential one-on-one coaching sessions with our Dream Manager, Alastair Hill. So far, every single one of them has recommended it. <u>More here</u> Rosie Brown, MD, Cook

Help your people fulfil their dreams: Propellernet has a dream machine (an old bubble gum dispenser). People put what they'd love to do in a dreamball and – every so often- one gets drawn. The first two went to the world cup in Brazil. Another motorcycled round Africa. "We literally make our people's dreams come true." Nikki Gatenby

Have a secret "angel" for "love week": At Malaysian company MindValley the aim is to make every member of staff feel valued and working in a way that aligns with their personal vision. One example is "<u>love week</u>", where every member of staff gets a secret "angel" whose role is to make them feel loved.

Discover the "3 potatoes of workplace happiness": is the key to happiness at work ensuring people are doing "what I do well", "what I love" and "what is useful"? Laurence Vanhee, ex-CHO, Belgian Ministry of Social Security

> "It's not rocket science. Happy people do better work than miserable people"
>
> Nikki Gatenby, Managing Director, Propellernet

Material Benefits

Buy a holiday home for your staff to use: Cook, who make "remarkable frozen ready meals", bought a holiday home in Kent at a cost of £80,000 and provides it free to staff. "It is especially popular with our lower paid staff and it's great to be able to give people a good break", explained Alison Payne.

> "No one should be more than two hundred feet away from food"
>
> Sergey Brin, Google founder (Work Rules)

Renovate houses to create homes for your staff: Housing is hard to buy in Brighton, especially with the competition from people moving down from London. So search marketing agency Propellernet decided to buy up run down properties, renovate them and sell them to staff. "This has been life changing for some of our people and hasn't even cost us anything. We sold some of the flats on the market and actually made money from the activity."

Share the wealth: John Lewis' profit share varies up to 15% of annual salary. "It can make a real difference to partners (as staff are called). You don't have to be a mutual to share the profit." Sarah Gillard, Director, John Lewis Partnership

Let peers set your bonus: Carrie Brandes, VP of people at Ubiquity (a California pensions advisory company) explained how they set bonuses. Everybody in the company is given 100 pts and can award however they see fit to whoever they feel has made an impact to the business or the company. Each person gets a bonus based solely on these peer ratings.

Let peers give awards: At Google, any employee can give anyone else a $175 cash award, with no management oversight or sign-off required. (from Work Rules)

Receive $200 from the company to thank a colleague: Frederick Laloux describes how, at Ozvision, each employee can take an extra day off each year, described as "day of thanking." They receive $200 in cash from company funds that they can spend however they want to thank a colleague during that day." (Laloux)

£5 from your peers: All members were given a supply of £5 M&S vouchers. These could be given to any other person who'd been co-operative and helpful. Dom Monkhouse, F**K Plan B

Simple things make a difference: "We asked staff what was annoying them. The biggest thing was that we had removed tea and coffee. It was 5 years previously, but still clearly an issue!. So we reinstated it and it has made a difference." Polly Neate, CEO, Shelter

Trust based HR policies: "Our people now have unlimited holidays, choose their own working hours and have self-regulated sickness, fully paid. As this approach can lead to people taking fewer vacations, we included a minimum number of days holiday. 'Have fewer rules and trust the team.'" Luke Kyte, Head of Operations, Reddico

Duvet Days: At Possabilities staff who have 100% attendance get an extra day off

Day off on your birthday: Common in many organisations, including Trinity, Impetus and Adviza. "It is very popular" explains Trinity CEO Steve Hedley

£500 for mental health support: We make available £500 to everybody for mental health support. They put it through on expenses, not even need to go through line manager. It can be for them or for their family. Helped a lot with older care and with their kids using it. Simon Biltcliffe, CEO, Webmart

Disability Leave: "we're introducing disability leave so disabled colleagues who need to go to appointments for eg new wheelchair, new personal assistants, that wouldn't fit under normal sick leave", Sarah Pugh, CEO, Whizz Kidz

Replace appraisals

"Like so many CEOs and CHROs are discovering, there's no evidence anywhere in the world, in any institution of management science, that existing massive employee evaluation and rating processes are effective." Jim Clifton, Jim Harter (It's the Manager)

Appraisals can make performance worse: Traditional performance appraisals are so bad that they actually make performance worse about one-third of the time. (Quoting this from Gallup)

$1 billion wasted by appraisals: One large global professional services company estimated that it was wasting $1 billion of leadership time per year on managers filling out ratings forms rather than developing employees and having ongoing coaching conversations with them. (It's the Manager)

Abolish appraisals: They don't make people happy and don't serve any useful purpose. "You hear managers saying I'll feedback at their appraisal in two month's time, rather than now when its needed. Replace appraisals with coaching and one-to-ones. You move from something nobody likes to something they do". Sophie Bryan

"Who can remember what they've done across a whole year? What's the point of telling someone that they've under-achieved for 12 months?" Dom Monkhouse, F**k Plan B

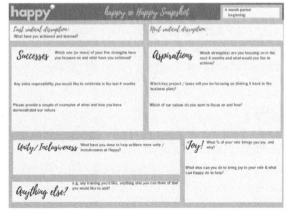

Get staff to vote on appraisals: "After a staff vote we got rid of appraisals and replaced them with a one page snapshot reviewed at a four-monthly check-in." **Cathy Busani, Managing Director, Happy**

Ask about Joy: Ask: "what would give you more joy?", instead of "how can we improve your performance?"

Annual feedback from your colleagues: At Morning Star, people receive feedback at the end of every year from each of the persons they have committed to in their CLOU (Colleague Letter of Understanding, where Morning Star staff make commitments to their colleagues).

Abolishing appraisals in a local authority: In 2018 Hackney Council (in East London) abolished appraisals for all 4,000 staff. They replaced them with regular one-to-ones and quarterly check-ins.

"Our research has suggested that the Check Ins have helped staff members take ownership of their goals and objectives and to think of new ways of achieving them. The most valuable part of the conversation has been the opportunity that they have to talk to their managers about anything (and everything!) that has been happening for them over the past 4-6 weeks in a safe and open space and feel like they are genuinely being listened to." Emily Cooper

Peer evaluation over dinner: At AES, Dennis Bakke installed a practice of team appraisal with his closest peers. They got together once a year, often over dinner in one of their homes to make for a relaxed, informal setting. Every person in turn shared his or her self-evaluation. Other team members commented, questioned, or encouraged each other to reach a deeper understanding of their potential and performance.

Peer feedback at Netflix: Netflix seeks for people to give clear and direct feedback. They use the approach of "Stop, Start, Continue" and each team gets together over supper to feed back to each other on how they each are doing. (No Rules Rules)

Buurtzorg: the team decides how to evaluate each other: the rules of the game simply stipulate that every year, each team is to hold individual appraisals within the team, based on a competency model that the team has designed. Each team decides what format it will use for their discussions. A team I spent time with decided to exchange feedback in subgroups of three colleagues. Everyone prepares a self-evaluation as well as feedback for the other two colleagues in the trio, so people can measure their self-perception against their colleague's perceptions. (Laloux)

Recognition

Morning praise and thank you: "ESBZ, the grade 7-12 school in Berlin, has an extraordinary trust and community-building practice based around storytelling: the "praise meeting." Every Friday afternoon, the entire school—students, teachers, and staff—comes together for an hour in a large hall. They always start by singing a song together, to settle into community. All the rest of the time together is unscripted. There is an open microphone on stage, with a simple rule: we are here to praise and thank each other." (Laloux)

Share customer delight: At Zappos they created a WhatsApp group called 'Moment of WOW'. All staff are a member of it and whenever they get great feedback, or do something good for a customer, they share it here. (quoted in Leading with Happiness)

Recognise the assist: "There is a US basketball team where the manager requires anybody who scores to point at the person who helped them, to recognise the assist. At the start of meetings we used to ask for a win. Now we ask for an assist, something somebody has done to help them." Russell Findlay, CEO, Speakers Trust

Staff first, customers second

> If you want to WOW the customer, first you must WOW the people who WOW the customer. Tom Peters, Extreme Humanism

Make engagement as important as margins: "Happy, engaged staff perform better so focus on engagement to get the results you want." Nikki Gatenby

Employees First, Customers Second: That is the title of the book by Vineet Nayar, then CEO of 150,000 strong Indian outsourcing company HCL.

The customer comes second: This book, by Hal Rosenbluth & Diane Peters, was a key influence on Happy in its early days. Just before publication, Rosenbluth Travel had won the Baldrick award for the best customer service in the entire USA. Henry describes the core message as "hire nice people and treat them well."

> "Your employees come first. There's no question about that. If your employees are satisfied and happy and inspired by what they are doing, then they make your customers happy and they come back. We tell our people, 'Don't worry about profit. Think about customer service. 'Profit is a by-product of customer service."

Challenge

> "The American psychologist Theodore Isaac Rubin put it like this: Happiness does not come from doing easy work. It comes from the afterglow of satisfaction after the achievement of a difficult task that demands your best."
>
> Alexander Kjerulf, Leading with Happiness

Leaving Well

A farewell meal for those leaving: When a person leaves CC&R, team members join together for a meal with the person who is leaving. "Everybody comes prepared with a personal story about that person's time with the organization", explains Frederick Laloux. "Of course, the stories are meant to celebrate the person who is leaving." (Laloux, Reinventing Organisations)

The company that never fires people for poor performance: Several years ago NextJump founder Charlie Kim said that he regarded his employees as like family. One responded by asking if he would fire a member of his family if they behaved badly. Charlie came in the next day and announced that, from then on, nobody would be fired from Next Jump for poor performance.

"It has had some unintended consequences", explained Tarun Gidoomal, London Managing Director. "First, it means you have to be very careful in who you hire. Virtually the whole team now has to agree before we appoint somebody as we know it's a job for life. Second, people have opened up more, and been prepared to share their stories, their faults and failures because there is no risk of getting fired. And it's led to people being more prepared to take healthy business risks."

5. Case Study: Happy

Happy helps organisations create happy, productive workplaces. We do this through a mixture of delivering learning and consultancy. It is important to us that we model what we are trying to create, based on the principles in the Happy Manifesto.

Create Joy at Work

The aim at Happy is for every person to find joy in their work at least 80% of the time. And we measure it (at the four-monthly check-ins). Our latest figure is an average 76%.

Play to strengths: A key element in finding that joy is, we find, doing stuff you are good at. At Happy, we recruit to a job description and then throw it away (or, rather, we have team job descriptions). Each of our people is encouraged to think about what they are, or have the potential to be, good at and how they can do more of it.

Managers as Coaches: Our "managers" used to be called co-ordinators and, after a staff vote, are now called M&Ms (mentors and multipliers). It is very clearly understood that their role is not to tell people what to do, or demonstrate their expertise, but to coach and help people find their own solutions.

> "I love my sessions with Cathy. I always leave my one-to-ones more excited and inspired than when I went in." Lydia Theaker

Separate the roles of managers: At Happy we have five heads of department. Some are also M&Ms, coaching their people. Some are not. The roles of thinking through the needs of that department are separated from the role of supporting, challenging and coaching people.

Choose your manager: New starters are allocated an M&M. After three months, however, they can choose whoever they want. People choose their managers at Happy, remembering that the role of a manager is to coach.

Transparency in action: Everything from the company finances to individual salaries are public at Happy. We do everything we can, including using lego, to help people understand the company finances. And all our people can look up everybody's salary (now and at every stage since the joined the company) in a simple spreadsheet.

Trust people: The aim is that everybody is trusted to make decisions in their area, within whatever guidelines are appropriate. As boss of the company, my aim is to make no decisions as boss of the company, but to create the environment for others to step up, normally those closest to the decision point.

Celebrate Mistakes: I know that one of the things that people appreciate at Happy is the fact that if they take a risk, try something new, and it goes wrong we will celebrate the mistake.

Recruit for attitude: We never ask for qualifications, avoid CVs and seek to recruit for attitude, get people to do the job in the interview and hire collaboratively.

For facilitators we recruit in groups of six, so we can see how they interact and whether they are positive and supportive of each other. We deliver learning to them, so they are clear on what is needed and then ask them to facilitate with each other. While we throw in one or two challenges (such as taking them aside in the 2nd interview to be coached, and then seeing if they change), we do not at any point ask them any questions.

Overall, our aim is to create a fulfilling workplace where people are trusted and can work at their best.

6. Give freedom within clear guidelines

I have asked thousands of people whether they prefer "being told what to do", "complete freedom" or "freedom within guidelines". The answers are consistent and vary little between sectors or even between levels of seniority. Very few (under 2% in my experience) want to be told what to do. Some, especially entrepreneurs and CEOs, like complete freedom.

However I find that over 90%, in nearly all environments, want "freedom within guidelines". They want to know the framework they are working within, but then be trusted to use their own judgement. People want to know what is expected of them. But they want freedom to find the best way to achieve their goals.

> "Freedom + responsibility leads to happiness and performance. That's the equation we used to transform the Belgian Ministry of Social Security." Laurence Vanhee, ex-CHO, Belgian Ministry of Social Security

Give full autonomy to make decisions: At Mayden staff are expected to go through a framework of 7 questions and then, if they feel the decision fits them, can make the decision themselves, including spending. Chris May, Mayden.

Let your people decide: "As responsible adults we let our team choose: Where. When. How they work." Laurence Vanhee

Give your staff flexibility in decisions. "At Timpsons the price list is only a guide. Staff can charge what they want", John Timpson

> "Responsible people thrive on freedom and are worthy of freedom. Our model is to increase employee freedom as we grow,

rather than limit it, to continue to attract and nourish innovative people, so we have a better chance of sustained success."

Reed Hastings, Netflix founder (Work Rules)

Building ownership

Set up your own Leadership Team at Nearsoft: At the Mexican software company staff can set up a Leadership Team in response to a perceived issue. One example was year-end bonuses, which some felt weren't fair. The Leadership Team – set up by members of staff - proposed changes, tested it out and, after refinement, implemented the new approach across the organisation. (Worldblu, 50 transformation practices)

Get people to set their own targets

If your people are motivated and feel in control, they are likely to set tougher targets than managers, to feel better about them and be more likely to achieve them.

The one minute target at GCHQ: GCHQ is the government's intelligence and security organisation. The Head of IT describes how, after reading the Happy Manifesto, he let his people set their targets. "We have found that if you let people set their own targets, they set tougher targets and are more likely to achieve them."

He gave the example of their tech support people. With security concerns at the forefront, it used to take two weeks to check out a laptop. "It was clear we needed to shorten it. If it had been left to me to set the target, then I would have probably set it at one day – a huge improvement on where we were. We left it to the team. They set the target at 5 minutes. When they achieved that, they reduced it to two minutes. They have now got it down to one minute." (Spark the Change Conference, 2016)

Use direct feedback to help people set targets: At Happy I sat down with Natalie, who had just taken over credit control, to agree targets. At the time we were owed £135,000. Instead of setting a target, I asked Natalie to send me a spreadsheet every fortnight, showing how much we were owed in total, at 30 days and at 90 days – key information I needed.

I then asked her to set her targets for the next report. The first time she set a very low figure and didn't make it. The second, she was conservative and overachieved it. As time went on, she became clearer and also became very focused on achieving the target she had set. By the time she left to go on maternity leave the amount owed had dropped to £35,000, less than it had been in years.

Collective objectives: "Individual objectives are bullsh*t. We got people to set collective objectives, to work towards together, and productivity increased by 20%." Laurence Vanhee, ex-CHO, Belgian Ministry of Social Security

At Geonetric, staff "map their choices": Quarterly, each team reviews Geonetric's overall priorities, and creates a team Impact Map of how they will contribute. In turn each individual creates their own Impact Map. They choose, for each of the team's goals, whether they want to lead the initiative, provide support, or provide advice during the process—and to what level? (Worldblu, 50 Transformational Practices.)

Let teenagers set their own curfew time: In Becoming, Michelle Obama describes how her parents used guidelines rather than rules. As teenagers they never had a fixed curfew. "Instead they'd ask 'What's a reasonable time for you to be home?' and then trust us to stick to our word."

> "If you set a crazy, ambitious goal and miss it, you'll still achieve something remarkable."
>
> Larry Page, Google founder, Quoted in Work Rules

Or have no targets at all

> "People with targets and jobs dependent upon meeting them will probably meet the targets, even if they have to destroy the enterprise to do it."   W. Edwards Deming

No targets, no goals? That is the approach at the successful software company Basecamp. "You can absolutely run a great business without a single goal. You don't need something fake to do something real. And if you must have a goal, how about just staying in business? Or serving your customers well? Or being a delightful place to work? Just because these goals are harder to quantify does not make them any less important. We don't do grand plans at Basecamp—not for the company, not for the product. There's no five-year plan. No three-year plan. No one-year plan. Nada.

"Every six weeks or so, we decide what we'll be working on next. And that's the only plan we have. Anything further out is considered a "maybe, we'll see." The sooner you admit you have no idea what the world will look like in five years, three years, or even one year, the sooner you'll be able to move forward without the fear of making the wrong big decision years in advance."

"It doesn't have to be crazy at work", Jason Fried and David Heinemeier Hansson

Systems not Rules

> 94% of problems in business are systems-driven and only 6% are people-driven. —Attributed to W. Edwards Deming

Forget the manuals and policies: "Get your people to be more human at work and just do the right thing." Donna Reeves

Regularly attach the problem: At Google there is an annual program called Bureaucracy Busters where Googlers identify their biggest frustrations and help fix them. (Laszlo Bock, Head of People, Google in Work Rules)

Just one rule at Nordstrom: US department store Nordstrom, famous for its customer service, issues new employees with a card stating its one rule: "Use good judgement in all situations. Please feel free to ask your department manager, store manager, or human resources officer any question at any time." (McCrystal)

'Make a Friend' instead of processes and call handling times: At United Utilities they moved from call scripts and measurement of call handling times. "Instead", explained Customer Services Director Louise Beardmore, "I said to people you are all adults and I want you to talk to customers like they are friends."

"The step change that we have seen in performance is immense. I am averaging about 140 to 160 thank you's or wow awards from customers who have spontaneously given me feedback about employees." (From 2017 Happy Workplaces conference)

"We have no idea what your venture is or even your industry, so we won't presume to tell you how to create a business plan. But we can tell you with 100 percent certainty that if you have one, it is wrong." Eric Schmidt (How Google Works)

Innovation

At GCHQ there is one day a month set aside for innovation: The status quo is set aside. Using a dedicated collaborative space to promote new thinking, where posters are presented, workshops are run and experts from the community come to talk about their fields. One talk is all about failed projects. The community embraces "fail fast" and mistakes are celebrated as learning points for the individual but also corporately. Each day has a theme with a challenge designed to inspire new collaborations throughout the day.

The introduction of innovation days took the proportion of staff actively engaged in innovative projects from 18% of the workforce to 82%. A key target of the days is finding more efficient ways to do previously manual tasks. For one highly disruptive project (changing how fundamental processes are followed at the core of GCHQ) it resulted in halving costs and a 32% reduction in time to completion. More here

> "If you know where you're heading, you're not innovating. If things work out as planned, you weren't chasing anything interesting."
>
> Tom Peters, The Excellence Dividend

Ask your customers: The Arsenal food store is a convenience shop close to the football club's Emirates Stadium in North London. It won a local customer service award based on one simple method. The owner asks people who come into the shop what they would like that isn't stocked there already – and orders it.

A simple and obvious step. But have you ever been asked in any shop what you would like them to stock? How often do you ask that question of your customers?

> 'In a company born to innovate, the risk is not innovating. The real risk is to think it is safe to play safe.'
>
> Jony Ive, Chief Design Officer, Apple   (quoted in Winners, Alistair Campbell)

Feedback

Use peer feedback: "Research has shown peers have twice as much impact as anything your manager does", Alison Stugess-Durdon, Director, Mayden

Let people own the metrics: The key metric for a training business is trainer utilisation (how much of the cost of a course goes on the trainer). As we moved to embed the Happy culture, trainers were now asked to take full responsibility and complete a simple spreadsheet each month to report back on their utilisation.

It produced a new focus for them and for support staff, giving them the key information they needed. As a result the proportion of trainer cost fell from 42% to 29% (on its own more than doubling the level of profit across the business).

Decide when you want feedback: At Indian outsourcing company HCL, employees can ask for feedback using the EPIC (Employee Passion Indicative Count) survey. This evaluates employee passion, motivating factors and personal strengths. But it is up to the individual to decide whether they want the feedback and when to make it happen. {Worldblu, 50 transformational practices)

Choose your questions and who you want to hear from: This is a neat idea from Aaron Dignan in Brave New Work. Ask each member of your team whether they'd like feedback, whether they'd like to sue standard questions (such as stop/start/continue) or choose their own. And who they would like to receive feedback from.

"Send the questions to their suggested colleagues with a time limit for contribution. Make this a ritual that is prioritized and celebrated in the culture. Compile and share the responses with each participant. Let them choose who to share it with, including their manager (if they have one)."

"A company's job isn't to empower people; it's to remind people that they walk in the door with power and to create the conditions for them to exercise it. Do that, and you will be astonished by the great work they will do for you."

Patty McCord, Chief Talent Officer, Netflix (in Powerful)

7.   Case Study: Cook

COOK was founded in 1997. It's a quality frozen food business that cooks food and sells it in shops on the high street. This, along with their e-commerce and home delivery operations, amounts to a workforce of about 1,200.

Relationships have been at the centre of the company since day one. It's certainly not the easy way, says Rosie: "Leaning into relationships and working with humans and our egos can be a messy, challenging business." But this hasn't stopped COOK from prioritising relationships.

Not only are strong relationships the basis of wellbeing, but they're also the most vital contributor to human happiness. "The longest running study of happiness ever is the Harvard Grant Study," says Rosie. "It's taken seven decades and its conclusion is really clear, which is our sense of happiness and fulfilment across a lifetime depends on the warmth of our relationships with others."

Relationships don't just buttress contentment – they help people to thrive, both inside and outside of work. This is something COOK has learned through its scheme to help put people with barriers to employment back into work. And from a commercial standpoint, the data clearly indicates that when a shop team has good relationships, the shop performs better.

There's no imbalance in terms of how COOK approach commercial strategy and how they approach relationship; each is pursued with serious intent. They've identified three key things to cultivate and nourish great working relationships. "They need common purpose, they need clarity and they need appreciation," says Rosie.

Common purpose ensures that when things get tricky and relationships start to fray, there's something to come back and build from. Beyond this, every year COOK runs a culture collective event where 200 team leaders take two days out to gather and reflect on why they're doing what they're doing.

Clarity means understanding how to use one's skills to contribute to successful operations. When clarity is lacking, that's when political disputes arise and relationships break down.

The Importance of Appreciation

Rosie identifies appreciation as the most important element of all. "We want to be appreciated for what we're bringing to the party and that in turn makes for better relationships," she says. COOK has a commitment to meet the needs of those working in the organisation. This is demonstrated in a variety of ways, such as financial wellbeing workshops, mental health and confidence workshops, and English workshops for the Eastern European workforce.

"At individual, team and company level, when we have common purpose, we have clarity on our contribution and we appreciate and feel appreciated by those we're working with, we're well on the way to good working relationships," says Rosie.

8.   Be Open and Transparent

> "Without information you cannot take responsibility.
> With information you cannot avoid responsibility."
> Jan Carlzon, CEO, SAS Airlines (1981–94)

Share everything: When Darren Childs became CEO of UKTV, he reduced the barriers between leaders and employees by sharing information about the company's finances, the performance reviews of the leadership team. He also allowed all employees to ask him anything they wanted at their weekly Town Hall staff meetings, with all questions added to a box that was opened on stage at the meeting.

Share the financial information: "At WL Gore we've got a core value which is belief in the individual and we believe that everybody walking into work wants to do a good job. We place trust immediately you walk in the door. So if someone comes into the door and they want to know what the financial situation is, as a leader I'll say: 'Yeah, this is it, this is where we're at.' "

We're very open with information, we trust people. Because if you haven't got the information, how can you make decisions? (John Housego at the 2016 Happy Workplaces conference)

Share and people take responsibility: In 2012 I was away from the office and somebody asked our Finance Manager what the bank balance was. She knows we share all information so she told them. Then they asked how much it was a month before and three months before. As they delved more deeply it was clear there was a serious problem.

By the time I got back in the office, just a few days later, they had formed an action group to deal with it and had already identified tens of thousands of pounds of potential savings. That taking of responsibility was a key moment in turning Happy round at a key moment

Invite union reps (or staff representatives) to all senior management meetings: Paul Wakeling, Principal at Havering Sixth Form College, explained how it took a lot of support and work to put this into practice but feels it has paid off in terms of more inclusiveness and better decisions. "Especially when you say something you think is uncontroversial and you see a reaction. And you know, if you'd gone ahead, that would have been the reaction of people across the organisation."

Move competence down to the front line: "Take Morningstar, the world's largest tomato processor. It has no managers and all key investment decisions are taken by individuals who in other organizations would be regarded as "blue collar" employees. Most of these employees are capable of sophisticated financial modelling—they can calculate the net present value and internal rate of return of new investments.

Instead of moving decisions upward at Morningstar, they have moved competence down—to individuals who have the information and the context to make the best decisions." (Age of Agile, Stephen Denning)

Leave open seats at your executive meetings: Learning from Paul's example at Havering, we decided to leave two seats open to staff on a first-come, first-come first served basis. Anybody can now attend the Happy Senior Leadership Team meeting, which takes place for an hour, once a month.

Make all manager plans public: Previously at HCL the 300 most senior managers had prepared their plans for the next level up. Instead the company published them all to all staff in the MyBlueprint portal, so they could see and compare them. As well as increasing transparency, CEO Vineet Nayar comments that it led to much more work being put into getting the plans right.

Share your CEO Problems: At HCL Vineet Nayar decided to create a portal to share the problems he was having difficulty solving as CEO and the challenges he saw for the company. He involved the whole company in understanding his role, the big picture and in coming up with solutions. (from Employees first, customers second)

> Our standing guidance was "Share information until you're afraid it's illegal."
>
> General Stanley McChrystal, Team of Teams

If the data is clear and public, people want to improve: At Dutch care company Buurtzorg, where the nurses are organised into teams of ten to twelve, the productivity of each team is listed regularly in a table. "Teams at the bottom are motivated to improve out of pride; they don't need a boss to discuss how they could improve", explains Frederick Laloux. (Laloux, Reinventing Organisations)

Full transparency at HCL: The Indian conglomerate HCL introduced full transparency of the performance of every unit in the company. Seeing their benchmarks, and being able to compare their performance with others, increased shared learning and provided powerful incentives to improve.

At Nucor employees are responsible for maximising margins: "Nucor, the most consistently profitable steel company in the world, practices radical transparency. Every single associate knows the profitability of every order that ships. At Nucor, it is the frontline employees, not managers, who are responsible for maximizing margins." (The Age of Agile, Stephen Denning)

Financial Literacy at New Belgium Brewing: After workers answered 50% when asked what percentage of income went to profit, the company introduced open-book finances. Now there are finance classes – including how to read profit-and-loss reports

- and updated at each monthly meeting. {Worldblu, 50 transformational practices)

> "Assume that all information can be shared with the team, instead of assuming that no information can be shared. Restricting information should be a conscious effort, and you'd better have a good reason for doing so. In open source, it's countercultural to hide information."
>
> Laszlo Bock, Head of People, Google in Work Rules

Communication

Floor to Board in 5 minutes: Liz Mouland is Chief Nurse at First Community, and recalls: "We wanted to design something that was not non-hierarchical but was an inverted hierarchy. We see the function of the Board and of management is to support those providing excellent care and services to the public.

"One example of how we do this is our 'Floor to Board in five minutes'. Any of our 450 staff can contact a Board member within five minutes. Out of hours they can use the 24/7 On Call Manager phone number who can escalate to a Board member if appropriate."

Remove the door from your office: Another is the organisation's open-door policy. Liz, as clinical lead for the organisation, literally has no door on her office. "We have a behaviours framework which we expect everybody to role model. It is about showing emotional intelligence, with warmness and friendliness, where everybody's voice matters."

Remove the wall from your office: The new CEO at UKTV wanted to reduce the barriers between leaders and staff, so one if his first acts was to take the walls off his office.

Brutal Honesty at Mindvalley: Each week at this Malaysian education company CEO Vishan Lacklani conducts a "Brutal Honesty" session. Employees can anonymously ask any question they want and the founders must answer them openly and authentically. It is said to create a climate of healthy dialogue, deep listening and trust. (Worldblu, 50 transformational practices)

Simon Perriton, Just IT: Open Forum: A space where people can ask anything and get answers from senior management.

Tell Me, direct link to Director at United Utilities: "I introduced this thing called Tell Me. You can tell me anything you want to tell me, any day. You can tell me if you are fed up. You can tell me if I am doing something stupid. There is not a form; there is not a process. I have an email address for Tell Me. They come through every day – between 40 and 45 every single day. They are everything from 'Louise, why does it say this on the bill because that telephone number isn't right'. Or 'Louise, I spoke to a customer today and actually I think it would be better if this tariff were designed in this way'. Or 'Louise I am hacked off because I have just been given my holiday allocation and I don't like it'.

"So what is your mechanism for hearing your employee voice and how complicated have you made it? Because if it is complicated or it's a case of I tried to tell you once but nobody did anything, then I am not going to bother again."

Louise Beardmore, Customer Services Director, United Utilities, 2017 Happy Workplace conference

Try two minute Tuesday: "Every Tuesday I record a two minute video on what's going on, and distribute it to all our people. The good stuff and the difficult stuff.", Derek Hill, MD, ATS,

What colour are your balls? At Dreamhost, a container at the exit contains red, yellow and green balls. Every member of staff places a ball when they leave the office (green for great day, red for bad, yellow for in the middle). The number of balls of each colour is recorded each day at each location. Those leaving Red are encouraged to leave a note of explanation, which the leadership reads daily. (Worldblu, 50 transformational practices)

Everyone must have the freedom to communicate with anyone at Pixar: This means recognizing that the decision-making hierarchy and communication structure in organizations are two different things. Members of any department should be able to approach anyone in another department to solve problems without having to go through "proper" channels.

It also means that managers need to learn that they don't always have to be the first to know about something going on in their realm, and it's OK to walk into a meeting and be surprised. The impulse to tightly control the process is understandable given the complex nature of moviemaking, but problems are almost by definition unforeseen. The most efficient way to deal with numerous problems is to trust people to work out the difficulties directly with each other without having to check for permission.

https://hbr.org/2008/09/how-pixar-fosters-collective-creativity?utm_medium=social&utm_source=twitter&utm_campaign=hbr

Open Salaries

Publicly available salaries at Buffer: At the online software company not only are salaries available internally, but they publish them on their web site for all to see. Within the first month of posting this, Buffer doubled the number of job applicants they received

It's about fairness: At Glitch (previously called Fog Creek Software) all salaries are shared internally. "Transparency isn't the goal," explains Anil Dash, Glitch's CEO. "The goal is paying everyone fairly, and transparency forces us to do that." (here)

See every salary people have ever earned: At Happy we have a spreadsheet, which is available to anybody internally, which details both current salary and every salary people have ever earned at the company – together with the reasons for each increase. "Give people full information and they are more likely make good decisions", explains founder Henry Stewart

Internally available salaries: Companies at which staff can see everybody's salary include Piscina International, Whole Foods, Namaste Solar, CareerFoundry, Crowdfunder, SumAll and many more

9.   Case Study: Belgian Federal Office of Social Affairs

"How people feel and think determines their behaviour. So focus on making them feel good." Laurence Vannhee, ex-CHO

When Frank van Massenhove took over the Belgian Federal Officer of Social Affairs in 2002, he was determined to create freedom and responsibility for the employees.

One of his first steps was to allow employees to work when they want and where they want. Even before the pandemic there were typically only 150 people present in the office, out of a workforce of 1,070.

People are evaluated solely on the results, not on the number of working hours. Frank estimates that people work an average 30 hours a week, as does he.

Frank posed this question to the workforce: "How do we build a government department aimed at customer satisfaction and results-driven work, where the employees are happy?"

"The goal was to make civil servants happy and create a more efficient government", Frank explains in "Making Work Fun" the book by Corporate Rebels.

The book describes how "productivity rose by 18% during the first three years, and after that by an average of 10 percent per year. The ministry has the lowest number of illness-related absences in Belgium, and there is virtually no burnout".

Or as Laurence Vanhee, who was Chief Happiness officer at the Department, described it at the 2018 Happy Workplace conference: "Productivity rose 20%, rental costs fell by 12 million euro, maintenance costs by 50%, spontaneous applications rose by 500%. Staff turnover fell by 75%"

Burn the Box

"Don't just think outside the box, burn the box", explains Laurence. "When we brought in flexible working the receptionists asked if they could work from home. We assumed that wouldn't work. But they teamed up with some of the admin staff, agreed a shared workload and got to work at home some days of the week. Think differently."

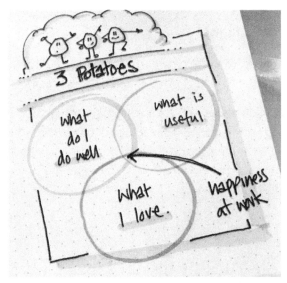

For Laurence crucial were the "3 potatoes of workplace happiness": "what I do well", "what I love" and "what is useful"?

"It is about trust: Move from command and control to trust of your people. Your leaders should be facilitators not experts."

Also, use Collective objectives: "Individual objectives are bullsh*t. We got people to set collective objectives, to work towards together, and productivity increased by 20%.

Freedom + responsibility lead to happiness and performance: "That's the equation we used to transform the Belgian Ministry of Social Security."

Kisssify the process: "Keep it sexy, keep it simple, keep it sustainable. If the process or policies don't fit that, get them changed."

Initially Frank changed from 5 levels of hierarchy to 2. Now a major section of the Department has become self-managing, as of April 2016.

Saskia Gheysens explains in a Corporate Rebels article: "We see that in the new structure people stand up and display talents we haven't seen before. They have more opportunity now to show their talent – they have really started to flourish."

Don't tell the politicians!

How did politicians react to these changes. Frank didn't tell them! "I kept my mouth shut until we achieved the necessary results."

However the proportion of civil service applicants wanting to work for the department has gone from 18% in 2002 to 93% now. And they now have 57 applicants, on average, for each vacancy – compared to 3 before the transformation.

10. Recruit for attitude, train for skill

Instead of qualifications and experience, recruit on attitude and potential ability. Use collaborative hiring and get people, as close as possible, to do the job in the interview.

Recruit for attitude

Google looks for people who are "Googly": "We look for a cultural fit with the company", explained Yvonne Agnei – then Google Head of Benefits – at the 2013 Happy Workplaces conference. This includes a passion for what you do, interests beyond work. "We like people who travel, we like people who speak more than one language and engage with their community. Now we don't hire people if we don't think they are "googly". If they mis-treated the receptionist or came across as arrogant, we would not hire them whatever their skills."

Hire for humility: at NextJump Many companies now say they "hire for attitude, train for skill". At Next Jump they hire for one specific attitude. "We used to screen for skills. And we ended up with a lot of brilliant jerks", explains joint UK Managing Director Tarun Gidoomal. "So now we hire for humility." In the two talks I've seen NextJump executives give that has been very evident. What has stood out has been both the humility and vulnerability they were prepared to show.

Recruit for personality at Timpsons. "We can teach them how to cut keys and repair shoes" explained Timpsons founder John Timpson

When Google learnt skills weren't enough: In a period of extreme growth, 2005-2008, there was a focus on hiring the right skills. In 2007 they realised they were having challenges in some of the people they'd recruited, picked up especially in the regular Googlegeist, the employee satisfaction survey. Google realised they had veered off in their hiring practice and had brought in senior people with a more command-and-control approach, "which doesn't work at Google at all." The response was to dramatically improve the induction process, to help people understand culture and weed out people who have a "tell" approach.

(From Yvonne Agnei's speech at the 2013 Happy Workplaces conference.)

Get the team to write the job description and set the salary: "Instead of the manager writing the job spec and setting the salary, we got the team to do it. They will be working with them and, as our salaries are transparent, they know what everybody else is earning and are best placed to decide the right amount for the new recruit." Cathy Busani, Happy

Make them fall in love with you! Finally, always be clear that the recruitment process should be as much about giving them a positive picture of your company (whether or not they get the job) as solely meeting your needs. As Laszlo Bock puts it: "Remember too that you don't just want to assess the candidate. You want them to fall in love with you. Really. You want them to have a great experience, have their concerns addressed, and come away feeling like they just had the best day of their lives."

But be wary of appointing people because you like them: "Truth be told, some of our most effective colleagues are people we most definitely would not want to have a beer with. (In a few rare instances they are people we would rather pour a beer on.)"

Eric Schmidt, ex-CEO Google (How google works)

Get people to do the job in the interview

Most interviews are based on questions. Candidates are asked how they performed well in a team or solved a problem, or whatever is needed for the job. The danger is that you will recruit somebody who is good at talking about how they would do the job, rather than good at doing the job. An alternative is to get people to perform the key tasks that are involved in the job.

Get them to do an actual real project in the interview: "At Basecamp we put a real project in front of the candidates so that they can show us what they can do. For example, when we're choosing a new designer, we hire each of the finalists for a week, pay them $1,500 for that time, and ask them to do a sample project for us. Then we have something to evaluate that's current, real, and completely theirs.

"It's the same kind of work they'd be doing if they got the job."

"It doesn't have to be crazy at work", Jason Fried and David Heinemeier Hansson

The best predictor is to get people to do a sample of work: In Work Rules, Laszlo Bock refers to the work by Frank Schmidt and John Hunter who in 1998 published a meta-analysis of 85 years of research on how well assessments predict performance. None of the methods fully predict but the single best predictor of how someone will perform in a job is a work sample test at 29%.

"We do our interviewing based on really testing your skills. Like, write some code, explain this thing, right? Not look at your resume, but really see what you can do."

Full day on the assembly line: At Toyota (see below), new recruits spend a full day on a fake assembly line.

Recruiting facilitators at Happy: We used to ask potential facilitators to explain what makes a great training session. Many would give a perfect explanation of a great session and then go on to delivery something completely different.

So now we don't bother with the first bit. We don't ask any questions of potential facilitators. Instead we get them to deliver a session. In the second interview, we take them aside and coach them and then get them to delivery again to see if they can learn.

Doing the job as a headteacher: As Chair of Governors of Stoke Newington School, I ensured that – when we recruited a new headteacher – they performed some of their key roles. The had to meet with students and parents. They held a management meeting with the two most difficult departments. And they ran a full staff meeting. And, in all those cases, we got all those involved to feed back.

We also had three formal interviews, as required by the local authority. The candidate who would have succeeded in those formal interviews was very different to the one who succeeded in the activities.

Collaborative Hiring

If only one or two people are involved in the recruitment, the danger is that they will recruit somebody like them.

Apple: Involve people from other parts of the business: At Apple you can easily interact with a dozen people in the recruitment process, any of which can be decisive. As Steve Jobs explained, "When we hire someone, even if they are going to be in marketing, I will have them talk to the design folks and the engineers."

Pret a Manger: the team decides whether to take them on: Once somebody has passed the initial screening at UK coffee and sandwich chain Pret a Manger, they work a day in one of the branches. At the end of the day all the staff in that branch take a vote on whether to take them on permanently. The aim is to find people who are "friendly and lively… people who are good-humoured by nature." And anybody who has been to Pret (I have a colleague who never goes anywhere else) will testify that they definitely succeed in finding those people.

Menlo Innovations: Make your partner look good: In what Inc described as the "The Most Unusual--and Effective--Hiring Process You'll Ever See" founder Richard Sheridan explains how they threw out the resumes, questions and fancy ads and instead hold mass auditions for people who will fit the culture.

Menlo is a coding company and, unusually, the programmers work in pairs (with just one computer). So the interviewees get to work in pairs, switching every 20 minutes and observed by Menlo staff. The team, not the managers, make the hiring decisions. And you get through if you show authentic collaboration, confidence and humility. As Sheridan puts it: "We explain to the candidates their goal: to make their pair partners look good enough to be invited back for the next stage of evaluation."

Involve the team and the clients: "For careers advisers and support workers we get the shortlist and they go out and meet the teams. We always involve young people too. Our people get the final say in who they will work with." Katherine Horler, Chief Executive, Adviza

Google: "Don't leave the interviewing to the bosses!": That is the advice of Laszlo Bock, Head of People at Google and author of the brilliant book "Work Rules". He explains that you may meet your future boss but far more important is to meet and be judged by those who will work for you, and also somebody with no connection to the job. "This sends a strong signal to candidates about Google being non-hierarchical, and it also helps prevent cronyism, where managers hire their old buddies for their new teams."

Facebook: Check the team dynamic: Julie Zhou, Director of Product Design, explains how Facebook likes to get a candidate to work with several other designers to evaluate the team dynamic.

They look over one another's work, provide feedback and get to see what they are like to work with in practice. Though they also have a major focus, as you might expect given their business, on how strong their online social presence is.

Zappos: the key is "culture fit": The US online shoe retailer Zappos is famous for its stunning customer service and for its policy of offering new hires $3,000 to leave at the end of their training. The idea is they only want people who want to work at Zappos enough to forego that offer. As well as those that interview them, candidates will go through a "social test" of attending some type of department meeting and getting others to interact informally with them.

Zappos also likes to send a car to pick up the candidate. Founder Tony Hsieh explains: "It doesn't matter how well the day of interviews went, if our shuttle driver wasn't treated well, then we won't hire that person."

Semco: Hiring by democratic vote: Brazilian company Semco was the original inspiration for the ideas of trust and freedom that we espouse at Happy. The company moved from being led from the top (and workers being searched each day at the gate as they left) to one where autonomous work teams had control over their job. This includes setting their own targets and production goals and also to hiring (and firing) both staff and supervisors by democratic vote.

Southbank Centre: Making it fun, interactive, and relevant: At the Southbank centre (the UK's largest arts centre), they used to recruit "hosts" using a traditional application form and interview. But then they realised that the hosts, who are the people who guide you around and show you to your seat, never have to write anything. So a process focused on how good their written answers were did not make sense.

Now they invite people in 200 at a time. The candidates get to find out about the South Bank, interact with each other and meet a whole range of staff. Those who are best with people get invited back, based on a wide range of staff views. They feel it's been much more effective. One interesting by-product is the people who get employed tend to be older than before.

Happy: I like to think we practice what we preach at Happy and seek to involve lots of people in the interview. We always interview candidates in groups, to see how people work together, and get involved those who will work with them. So for recruitment as a "smoothie" (short for Smooth Operator, the term chosen by our admin and customer service people after a night out dancing to Sade many years ago), every existing smoothie will get to sit in and have a say in who is chosen.

Try the pizza test: "We added an extra stage to recruitment where the new person meets their colleagues-to-be, maybe for pizza or another meal, to ensure the right fit. So far all have been accepted and it's really increased buy in." Luke Kyte, Reddico

Ask the team: "We needed a new HR manager, so we asked the HR team to go out and recruit and find two candidates they were happy with. They did all the pre-interviewing leaving me and my deputy to meet those final two. Rather than a formal interview, we just shared with them two difficult HR cases. The person we hired is a great fit for the organisation and compliments the other members of the team fantastically." Katherine Horler, Chief Executive, Adviza

Don't ask for qualifications

It doesn't matter how smart you are: "We don't pay too much attention to résumés. We are more interested in culture fit. We don't start with how smart you are. We don't care what you've learned. We aren't interested in where you've gone to college.

71

None of that matters if you don't fit our culture. Once we've determined that there is a fit with our culture, then we start to ask about skills." Richard Sheridan, Menlo Innovations (quoted in Age of Agile)

When Google required a degree and lost some of the most talented people in Silicon Valley: There was a crazy-strict rule in Product Management that you had to have a computer science degree to join the team. Many people wanted to transfer to Product because they had ideas they wanted to pursue, but they were prevented because they didn't have the right degree. One was Biz Stone who, stymied by the rule, left Google to cofound Twitter. Another was Ben Silbermann, who, similarly blocked, left Google to found Pinterest. Kevin Systrom also left Google to cofound Instagram when he couldn't join the PM team because of his college degree. (Kim Scott, Radical Candour)

(Google ex-CEO Eric Schmidt confirms this story in How Google Works. He describes how Salar Kamangar wanted to get Kevin onto the APM program. He argued that the young associate was a self-taught programmer and had a "history of working closely with engineers and shipping things". However others stuck to the degree rule, and denied the transfer, causing Kevin to leave and found Instagram.)

Ignore their education: On top of not considering provenance or location, we don't consider formal education, either. We look at people's actual work, not at their diploma or degree.

"It doesn't have to be crazy at work", Jason Fried and David Heinemeier Hansson

Google used to ask for degrees, until they did the research: Laszlo Bock, Google Head of People describes how in 2010 their "analyses revealed that academic performance didn't predict job performance beyond the first two or three years after college, so we stopped requiring grades and transcripts except from recent graduates."

"We now prefer to take a bright, hardworking student who graduated from the top of her class at a state school over an average or even above-average Ivy League grad", he says adding "some of our best performers never set foot on a college campus." (Work Rules)

Teach your people the required skills between the interview and starting work: In the airline industry it is normal for swimming ability to be a requirement for cabin crew. Virgin Atlantic noticed that this was restricting their ability to hire a diverse range of staff. So they kept the requirement but introduced swimming classes between interview and starting the job. https://www.virgin.com/richard-branson/changing-virgin-atlantics-cabin-crew-swimming-policy

Hire for kindness: "Don't hire for qualifications. We can teach them that. But we can't teach them to be kind and compassionate and to care. We find that out through scenarios, through discussions, trying to use more of those happy approaches." Katherine Horler, Chief Executive, Adviza

Qualifications often test the wrong stuff: At Happy we employed a young woman at the age of 16, who had no GCSEs at all. Three years later she became Finance Manager. And in all her time in that role she never had to calculate the angle on a triangle or solve a quadratic equation or do any of the other stuff involved in a Maths GCSE.

Induction

Send them champagne: One company described how they really want their new staff to feel valued. So a week before they arrive they send them a bottle of champagne and a pair of champagne glasses.

Send them flowers or a plant: At Happy, we know that won't be appropriate for everybody. So we send them flowers or a plant, again to make them feel appreciated.

Just send a card: "You talked about sending a card and flowers to new recruits before they start. We have a tight budget so we ditched the flowers and just send the card. It's a small gesture but it makes a real difference." Katherine Horler, Chief Executive, Adviza

Use your Fresh Eyes: "New staff can be a revelation. I search them out and ask what they've spotted, what doesn't seem right – before they've become too acclimatised", Nikki Gatenby, CEO, Propellernet

A little black book: "Every company since Rackspace, I'd give all new joiners a little black book. They were asked to write down anything they noticed that was annoying or stupid about the way we worked. I'd then meet them for lunch regularly during their first six months to discuss their ideas for change or improvement." Dom Monkhouse in "F**k Plan B"

Stop the inductions: "We stopped inducting people. Instead we got them to meet with their colleagues to share what you need to do to succeed and survive." Derek Hill, MD, ATS

Promotion

At WL Gore people promote themselves: When John Housego was asked, at the 2016 Happy Workplace conference, how people got promoted at WL Gore his answer was: "People step up and take on extra commitments".

"So because we take our own commitments we can promote ourselves every day, every year, at every opportunity. You've got to balance that around the whole work/life balance and whether you can deliver it or not, but self-promotion is how we grow in Gore and actually one of our core beliefs is a freedom principal: freedom to grow and develop and help others to grow and develop."

At Happy we didn't replace the Managing Director: When the Managing Director of our IT training business left we, influenced by the Gore example, decided not to replace him. Instead Henry said to staff "if you want to take on one of his responsibilities, go for it". A range of people stepped up to take on activities, while some of his tasks simply didn't continue. (At the next salary panel, people were rewarded for the tasks they took on.)

Moving people on

In the Happy Manifesto I describe the example of McKinsey who, when they know somebody isn't going to make Partner, encourage them to leave. But they give them several months and often find them work in one of their clients. As a result their ex-employees are devoted fans rather than disgruntled and resentful.

Help people leave: "If somebody isn't working out, help them to find what they want. We helped somebody leave and set up as a holistic therapy consultant. Now they come back and provide massages to our staff." Chris May, Director, Mayden

Netflix is not a family: Netflix does not see itself as a family but as like an elite sports team. There, you must pass the "keeper test" – as a manager, if this person were to leave, would you strive to keep them?

If they do not pass the keeper test, the manager is encouraged to let them go – with "a generous severance package". (Why is this in a book on Happy nickables? Because people prefer to work in a company where people are performing at their best.)

Get rid of the a**holes: "We just wanted team players in the Ministry of Social Security. We asked the a**holes to move to the Finance Ministry." Laurence Vanhee

11. Case Study: Toyota

"We build people before we build cars"

Despite its huge size, Toyota still includes many of these principles - including freedom to innovate, celebrating mistakes, hire for attitude. The Toyota Production System has made it one of the most innovative companies on the planet

12 ways in which Toyota create a great workplace

After visiting the Toyota engine plant in Deeside I wrote these reflections:

1: More people, less machines: The first surprise was that the assembly line was not full of robots. Most of the machinery looked as if it could have been in place 30 years ago. We were told that they have actually **reduced** the level of automation in recent years. "People are more flexible than machines" was one response.

There was also no SAP or ERP system in evidence. Instead the key monitoring tool was developed in Excel. "We want a system that adapts to the way we work, not to have to adapt to the way an existing piece of software works." And this was no paperless office. Charts and written sheets were everywhere.

2: Two improvements from each member every month: "Never be satisfied with what you have got" is a core principle at Toyota. Every "member" (as staff are called) is expected to come up with two "kaizens" (or ideas for improvement) each month. Indeed they are trained in fabrication and welding to enable them to be able to test out their ideas.

Time is dedicated to kaizen: Each member is allocated 15 minutes a day to identify possible improvements. Managers will try and avoid opposing a change, even if it has been tried before and not worked. A key point of kaizen is personal development: "The learning comes from the journey".

3: Intrinsic motivation, not money: There are no rewards for any financial gain resulting from the improvements people make. "We don't want our people driven by money but by the desire to improve the process." There are also no individual bonuses, only collective bonuses.

4: Standardise then improve: There is a sense of empowerment and engagement wherever you go at Toyota. But there is no sense of anarchy. Every process is carefully documented. "Every member is encouraged to improve the current process, but that standardisation makes it easy to return to the old process if the idea doesn't work." If the idea works, then the new approach is standardised and written down as a process by the member who created the improvement.

"Without standardisation there can be no kaizen" said Toyota founder Taiichi Ohno.

4: Each Toyota assembly line is different: When a new engine is created, or a new car rolled out, each plant will be equipped with the same assembly line and set of standardised processes. However each plant is continually innovating and, although Yakoten (sharing) means many innovations get adopted at other plants, some don't. The expectation that every member is continually seeking improvement means that every Toyota assembly line is different. There is standardisation of processes on each line but seems to be no desire for standardisation across sites.

The plant I visited on Deeside had a slightly old-fashioned look to it. But this is apparently the most productive Toyota assembly line on the planet, being the first to achieve an engine every 48 seconds.

5: Small changes matter: A kaizen doesn't have to be huge. One example was a lever that popped up a screw, meaning the member didn't need to bend down to pick it up. It was estimated to save two tenths of a second.

"We build ten million cars a year. Save two tenths of a second on each one and that's a gain of 560 person hours." Do one thousand of those a month (two for each of the 500 staff at the Deeside plant) and, if they are shared across the whole company, you've gained half a million person hours.

6: Quality Control Circles: Full involvement: Twice a month the assembly lines shut down for half an hour as every member gathers into their QCCs (Quality Control Circles). Here they study the data and learn more about what is going on in their section and throughout the company.

This may result in further improvements but "that is not the point. The aim is development" and that is what the carefully laid out QCC plans focus on.

7: A no blame culture: "We would never blame the individual. If something goes wrong, it is the process that has gone wrong." One of the two key pillars of the Toyota system is Jiduka. Every member can pull a cord to stop the belt if there is a problem, to help eliminate the root cause of problems.

Team leaders must never criticise a member for pulling the cord. "We want them to pull the cord". "If you blame somebody for failure, all that will happen is people will start sweeping problems under the carpet."

8: Systems to prevent error: I knew that Deming (the US management theorist that had such influence on Japanese methods) was clear that errors are caused by processes not by people. But visiting a Toyota assembly line really showed what he meant. Members will repeat the same process 150 times in a two-hour session. It would be easy to miss a step or use the wrong part if the process allowed it.

Many of the kaizen improvements specifically prevent that. Buckets have green lights which go off if a hand has reached in to collect a part, so you know if you've forgotten it. With one component it was too easy to pick up two, so the delivery was altered to physically prevent that.

The member we watched was working alternately on different engines with different spark plugs. If both types of spark plugs were available and the member picked the wrong set, that would not be "human error" but process error. So a plastic shield swings across between the two sets so only the correct one is uncovered. As backup (in case the shield fails) a green light goes on over the correct set of plugs. It is impossible to accidentally use the wrong plugs.

It is all fairly low tech but these are simple systems that prevent human error by making it as difficult as possible to make that error. This is known as "poka-yoke" or "mistake proofing" and is intrinsic to the Toyota approach. If your system allows somebody to make a mistake, it is the system that is wrong not the person.

9: It's all about the people: "Our greatest resource Is flexible, motivated members". Respect for people sits alongside continuous improvement at the core of The Toyota Way. "When you hire two hands you get a brain free. Clever people we have here,"

Managers are there to support. The development of the members is the most important thing you can do. "We build people before we build cars".

In the standard management diagram, the front-line staff are at the bottom and the top managers are at the top. At Toyota it is the other way round, clearly labelled that the role of managers is to support their members. They are expected to coach them and to ask "what can I do to help?".

10: Recruit for attitude, train for skills: "We can train people in the skills they need". They recruit for good communication, teamwork, willingness to improve. "It is not that they have the best skills but the right team fit."

11: Get them to do the job in the recruitment process: Those who know me will know this is my core requirement for effective recruitment. But Toyota take it to an extra level. Before they are invited to interview, applicants must spend a full day on an assembly line. Not the real one, but a mock assembly line. They are even asked to come up with one or two kaizen improvements at the end of it.

"We used to have people quitting on their first day, when they realised what they had to do. We don't get that any more. If they are not up to it, they quit on that mock day."

12: It's about people not money: One visitor asks if they have costed the time "lost" in working on kaizen and quality circles and compared it to the benefits that result and can show it makes financial sense.

The Toyota representative looks slightly baffled. It is one of those moments when you see two people working from completely different assumptions. It seems a calculation that Toyota would never see the need to carry out.

"We will never focus purely on cost", he explains. "Development of the members is the most important thing you can do, our biggest resource.

I left feeling that Toyota is truly a remarkable workplace. Those twin pillars of respect for people and continuous improvement seem genuine and embedded in everything they do.

The Toyota system came to widespread attention in the West when Womack and Jones of MIT wrote about it, defining it as "Lean Thinking". However their backgrounds meant they focused on the processes, such as cutting out waste, and largely ignored the people element.

It has even been said that founder Taiichi Ohno was very happy that the Toyota ideas had been so misunderstood in the West, by focusing on elements like the seven wastes, that were not actually the core element. (See "Did Toyota fool the Lean community?")

Deeside is the only Toyota plant in Europe that helps other organisations implement ideas like Lean and continuous improvement. But many organisations, they feel, are not able to be helped in this way. The NHS is one example. "Just too many restrictive practices".

The visit was part of the excellent Onsite Insights visits programme. Do contact them to find how you can get firsthand experience of great companies (including Happy).

12. Celebrate Mistakes

One of the things people like best at Happy is they know if try something new, possibly stretch themselves, and they do their best then they will never be blamed if it goes wrong. Indeed a no blame culture seems to be a feature of many of the most innovative organisations in the world.

> "Mistakes (WSTMSUW, whoever screws the most stuff up wins) are regularly celebrated (not 'tolerated') as essential steps on the path to progress; one successful CEO-innovator says he owes his success to a three-word motto: 'Fail. Forward. Fast.'"
>
> Tom Peters, The Excellence Dividend

Celebrate with wine and cheese: Michael Davies, Head of Sales at MacQuarie Telecom, told me of when he'd recently hired a yacht. He was told "If you get stuck on a sandbank call us out, and we will arrive with a bottle of wine and a cheese platter to celebrate."

Did he have to call them out? "Yes, twice". Both times the wine and cheese were brought. The reason was simple: Getting stuck on a sandbank isn't a problem if you know how to get off. If you don't, then you could wreck the underside of the boat. If something does go wrong, it's great to make sure that whoever fixes it, is the best person to fix it.

Intuit: "We celebrate failure": Accounting software company Intuit gives a special award for the Best Failure and holds "failure parties". "At Intuit we celebrate failure", explains co-founder Scott Cook, "because every failure teaches something important that can be the seed for the next great idea."

"It is not enough to 'tolerate' failure—you must 'celebrate' failure." Tom Peters, Extreme Humanism

Hold a party to celebrate:

Huntsman is a chemical company with a plant in North-East England. On the wall there used to be a big red button which, if pressed, discharged the chemicals into the local river. One day the scaffolders were in, and one of them nudged the button with his pole. His scaffolding company sacked him. But, when Huntsman found out, they insisted he be reinstated, sent back to work for them and even held a party to celebrate.

Nobody saw him press the button, but he had taken responsibility and gone to the control room and let them know. As a result it could be fixed in 30 minutes, rather than 24 hours, there was minimal environmental damage and no fine. "Holding that party sent a message round, and it spread like wildfire, that Huntsman is a no blame culture". If problems result from a mistake, it is rarely the mistake that causes it. More often, it is the cover up.

> "[Management guru] Peter Drucker provocatively suggested that businesses should find all the employees who never make mistakes and fire them because employees who never make mistakes never do anything interesting."
>
> Alexander Kjerulf, Leading with Happiness

Gore celebrates failure with beer or champagne: WL Gore, the makers of Goretex, was once voted the most innovative company in the US. They have long celebrated when a project doesn't work, with beer or champagne – "just as they would if it had been a success".

Gore's fundamental beliefs include: "action is prized; ideas are encouraged; and making mistakes is viewed as part of the creative process."

> "If we're not making mistakes, we're not trying hard enough."

Menlo Innovations: "Make mistakes faster": Make mistakes faster is a core principle at Menlo, the software company that founder Richard Sheridan set up to create a joyful work environment.

As my colleague Alex Kjerulf puts it (in a great post on celebrating mistakes), "They know that mistakes are an integral part of doing anything cool and interesting and the sooner you can screw up, the sooner you can learn and move on."

Netflix wants more failures: Netflix CEO Reed Hastings has worried that they have too many hit shows and not enough failures. Speaking at the 2017 Code Conference. "I'm always pushing the content team. We have to take more risk.

"You have to try more crazy things, because we should have a higher cancel rate overall." ("Netflix CEO Reed Hastings wants to start canceling more shows — here's why", Business Insider, 4/6/17)

Google: "reward failure"

In his book Work Rules!, Google's Head of People Operations Laszlo Bock states "it's also important to reward failure" so as to encourage risk-taking. Bock gives the example of Google Wave, an online platform launched in 2010 and closed a year later. "They took a massive, calculated risk. And failed. So we rewarded them."

Five thousand failures: James Dyson says he made 5127 prototypes of his vacuum before he got it right. That means 5126 were failures.

"If your goals are ambitious and crazy enough, even failure will be a pretty good achievement."

Tata: "Failure is a gold mine": Rajan Tata, founder and chairman of Indian conglomerate Tata created a prize for the Best Failed Idea, as he neared retirement. The aim is to spark innovation and keep the company from avoiding risks.

Failing Well is a programme at Smith College, Massachusetts: "What we're trying to teach is that failure is not a bug of learning it's the feature," explained Rachel Simmons, who runs the initiative. On enrolment, students receive a Certificate of Failure that declares they are "hereby authorized to screw up, bomb, or fail" at a relationship, a project, a test, or any other initiative that seems hugely important and "still be a totally worthy, utterly excellent human being." (On Campus, Failure Is on the Syllabus, New York Times, 24/6/17)

Celebrate at the Church of Fail: At Brighton-based social media company Nixon McInnes the Church of Fail is a monthly ritual. Employees are invited to stand and confess their mistakes, and are wildly applauded for doing so. "Making failure socially acceptable makes us more open and creative," says McInnes.

If people tell me they skied all day and never fell down, I tell them to try a different mountain." —Michael Bloomberg, Founder of Bloomberg

"Failure is an option": Dominos CEO Patrick Doyle gave a presentation to other CEOs empathising the need to avoid "omission bias" (avoiding a new idea in case it goes wrong and damages their career) and "loss aversion", the tendency to play not to lose: "The pain of loss is double the pleasure of winning." (Dominos stock price went up 30-fold under Doyle's leadership from 2009 to 2016.

(How Coca-Cola, Netflix, and Amazon Learn from Failure, HBR, Bill Taylor, 10/11/17)

"Make Mistakes faster": That is the principle at Menlo Innovations, who believe that it's not mistakes that threatens their progress but the fear of making mistakes. The believe that fast mistakes create the opportunity for quick feedback and rapid learning. (Worldblu, 50 transformational practices)

> "It is not enough to "tolerate" failure—you must "CELEBRATE" failure."
>
> Richard Farson, with Ralph Keyes, Whoever Makes the Most Mistakes Wins
>
> "We don't make mistakes at WD-40 Company, we have 'learning moments,' a positive or negative outcome of any situation that is openly and freely shared to benefit all."
>
> Garry Ridge, CEO, WD-40

Experimental culture at NextJump: "We try stuff out", explains Tarun. "Some of it works and a lot of it doesn't. To be honest, 60% of what we have done has failed. We have a saying that there are no OMGs, no mistakes ... only lessons learnt."

13. Case Study: Google

Some will regard Google as a controversial example. We know that it does not pay its fair share of taxes, it is seen as a key part of "surveillance capitalism" – monitoring our every move and there have also been staff protests in recent years.

However it has regularly won the best place to work surveys, both in the United States and internationally. And it is clear that the founders, Sergey Brin and Larry Page set it up with the belief that success would result from an empowered and fulfilled workforce.

How Google founder Larry Page learnt the importance of freedom at work:

In Radical Candour, Kim Scott explains a key influence: 'Shortly after I joined Google, Larry Page told me about a time when he'd had a boss who was suspicious of ambition. While on a summer internship, Larry had been given an assignment that would have taken him a couple of days if he'd been given the freedom to do it his way. He explained the advantages of his approach to the boss, but the boss would have none of it: he insisted that Larry do it "the way they'd always done it."

Instead of two days, Larry was forced to spend all summer working on the project. The wasted time and effort were pure torture for him. As most of us have, Larry discovered that a boss who held him back could make life miserable. "Three months of my life wasted and gone forever. I never want anyone at Google to have a boss like that. Ever,"' Kim Scott, Radical Candour

At Google being the boss doesn't mean you can tell people what to do

"Decisions really didn't get made by authority at Google—not even by the founders", explains Kim Scott in Radical Candour. At one point, Google's engineers decided to redesign the AdWords front end to make it easier for advertisers to choose different kinds of ad formats. Since most of Google's revenue came from AdWords, it was important to get this right. In one meeting, I watched Google cofounder Sergey Brin try to persuade a team of engineers to try his solution to the challenge of presenting to advertisers all the choices they had—different kinds of ad formats, different ways to make sure their ads showed up when and where they wanted, etc.—in the simplest possible way.

"The team proposed a different solution from Sergey's. He suggested that they put a couple of people working on his approach and let the rest of the team pursue their favoured solution. The team refused. Sergey, in a rare burst of frustration, banged the table and said, "If this were an ordinary company, you'd all be doing it my way. I just want a couple of people to try my idea!" He was clearly exasperated, but his grin showed that he was also proud of having built a team that would stand up to him. In the end, the team convinced him that theirs was the better way

> "Workplaces that permit employees more freedom tap into that natural intrinsic motivation, which in turn helps employees feel even more autonomous and capable."
>
> Laszlo Bock, Head of People, Google in Work Rules

At Google, people set their own targets: Yvonne Agyei, then Google Head of Benefits, made clear at the 2013 Happy Workplace conference that the Google approach is to let people set their own targets, within the overall goals. Every quarter the corporate strategy is revealed for the next three months.

"As a manager it is not your role to tell your people what they should be doing, rather it's a bottom-up process. Each Googler is expected to understand what the corporate objectives are and figure out how they contribute." Within three weeks of the whole company objectives being set, every one of the then 38,000 members of staff had set their own OKRs (Objectives and Key Results). Which means they each determine what they will be doing for the quarter.

At Google, targets are visible to all: In the Google directory, right next to a person's email and phone number are their OKR targets. This means, when contacting somebody, you can find out where their focus is and consider how what you want fits with that.

Weekly Town Hall meetings at Google: Every week Sergey and Larry hold TGIF (Thank God it's Friday), where they personally talk with hundreds of Googlers at the Mountain View HQ and thousands worldwide. They explain upcoming product launches, and share information on what the company is doing. Plus they take questions and "pretty much nothing is off limits". Googlers use simple online technology to vote questions up and down and decide what gets asked

Restrict what managers can do

"We deliberately take power and authority over employees away from managers. Here is a sample of the decisions managers at Google cannot make unilaterally: Whom to hire; Whom to fire; How someone's performance is rated; How much of a salary increase, bonus, or stock grant to give someone; Who is selected to win an award for great management; Whom to promote; When code is of sufficient quality to be incorporated into our software code base; The final design of a product and when to launch it." Laszlo Bock, Head of People, Google in Work Rules

Give people time to explore: In Work Rules, Laszlo Bock describes how, for 65 years, 3M has offered its employees 15% of their time to explore based on the core belief that creativity needs freedom. Products include Post-It notes and a clever abrasive material called Trizact, which somehow sharpens itself as it's used.

"Our version is 20 percent time, meaning that engineers have 20 percent of their week to focus on projects that interest them, outside of their day jobs but presumably still related to Google's work." (Note: There is some dispute about how much this is still in place and it does seem only to apply to engineers.)

> "What managers miss is that every time they give up a little control, it creates a wonderful opportunity for their team to step up, while giving the manager herself more time for new challenges."
>
> Laszlo Bock, Head of People, Google in Work Rules

Google's Dress Code: CEO Eric Schmidt was once asked at a company meeting what the Google dress code was. "You must wear something" was his answer (Eric Schmidt, How Google Works)

14. Community: create mutual benefit

Have a positive impact on the world and build your organisation too.

Supporting coding in local schools: Every branch of Next Jump is asked to adopt a local non-profit organisation. A particular focus is on schools. The New York office adopted PS119 in South Bronx, a school where 75% of the kids live below the poverty line. They funded the re-opening of the after school program (at a cost of $300,000 a year) to enable parents to continue to do their jobs uninterrupted, allow teachers to earn extra income, and students to have the extra support to grow and learn. Next Jumpers have been participating directly in the program, with every employee in the New York office spending a day a month helping build & teach a curriculum.

> "A company that can't figure out how to run their business in a way that makes the world better and happier shouldn't be in business at all."
>
> Alexander Kjerulf, Leading with Happiness

Use your core skills to help: With "Code for a cause" at NextJump, three people can take two weeks out to make a difference and scale and build a charitable project. One member of staff had a relation who had been in juvenile prison. She got together with two colleagues and spent the two weeks building tools for a charity helping ex-offenders.

Serve the wider community: The second biggest source of recruitment at Timpsons, after staff recommendation, is prison. The company not only recruits from people leaving prison, but has workshops within prisons to train up people for when they leave. They have recruited over 300 ex-prisoners. John Timpson: "We have 40 staff, including nine branch managers, who are still in prison - on day release."

> "I hired a corporate social responsibility person several years before I hired a sales person."
>
> Biz Stone, co-founder Twitter, Things a little bird told me

Does your company contribute to the community, four crucial tests:

1. Does your product or service make a positive contribution to society?
2. Do you treat your staff well and help them fulfil their potential?
3. Do you pay your suppliers within 30 days?
4. Do you pay your taxes?

If you can't answer Yes to these four questions, then the fact that you might contribute 1% of profit to charity is an irrelevance.

Purpose driven companies perform better: Socially conscious and purpose-driven companies featured by Professor and author Raj Sisodia in Firms of Endearment have outperformed the S&P 500 by a staggering 14x over a period of fifteen years, ten of which were after the publication of the book. (Aaron Dignan, Brave New Work)

15. Case Study: Haier

Haier is a Chinese white goods manufacturer employing 80,000 people, based on a non-hierarchical approach. It was introduced at the Thinkers50 London 2019 conference as "possibly the most innovative company on the planet." Corporate Rebels have described it as "The world's most pioneering company of our times."

Haier's CEO, Zhang Ruimin "We replaced the bureaucratic model with a model based on self-employment, self-motivation, and self-organization", explained Haier CEO Zhang Ruimin. "Our goal is to let everyone become their own CEO."

Zhang took over as General Manager of the Qingdao Refrigerator Plant in 1984, when it was close to bankruptcy. With a determination to focus on quality, one of his first acts has gone down in company legend.

Defective Fridges and Stunned Fish

After receiving a customer complaint about a defective fridge, he discovered 76 at the plant that had the same problem. He had them brought together in the centre of the factory, gave sledgehammers to the workers and had them destroy the faulty fridges (each then equivalent to two year's salary for a typical Chinese worker).

He expanded the company by buying up 18 rivals in a strategy called "revitalizing stunned fish" (the stunned fish being loss-making companies with poor leadership). He has continued this approach on the international stage, one of Haier's latest acquisitions being General Motors Appliances.

Haier has been described as "addicted to change". Over 30 years, Zhang has led the company thorough five strategic cycles of change, each transforming the culture of the organisation.

In 2012 Haier reorganised into small microenterprises, and eliminated 10,000 middle manager roles.

Self Organising Teams of 8

Speaking at the Thinkers50 conference in London in 2019, Zhang explained that Haier had split its 80,000 staff into units of 8. Instead of needing 13 levels of approval to spend, they now decide for themselves.

"Without management things are working out much better. Zero signature, zero approval." Growth went from 8% to 30% when they got rid of management.

Zhang was asked if any company can follow the Haier model? "Only if the CEO is prepared to give up 3 things: hiring & firing; salaries; making decisions. Are you prepared to trust your people?"

Crucial to Haier's approach is a focus on the customer, with the company's key platform being open to customers. As Zhang puts it: "In the past, employees waited to hear from the boss; now, they listen to the customer. "

16. Love work, get a life

The world, and your job, needs you well rested, well-nourished and well supported.

Improve your life balance

Put the phone down: "Average working hours have increased by 27% since we put emails on the phone. So put the phone away and stop using it for email." Nikki Gatenby

> "No distraction leads to quiet, quiet leads to flow, flow leads to progress, progress leads to satisfaction." Bruce Daisley, The Joy of Work

Wellbeing of your staff is important: John Lewis had a free at the point of service medical system for its partners (its staff) 20 years before the NHS was created. Sarah Gillard, Director, John Lewis Partnership

Google: Leave your laptop at the office: Although rated as a great place to work, Google has a notoriously long-hours culture. However even at Google, there are attempts to get people to work less and avoid burn out. In Work Rules, Laszlo Bock explains how Google Dublin introduced "Dublin goes dark", encouraging people to leave at 6pm, and providing drop-off locations for laptops, to prevent people working in the evening at home.

He quotes People Operations leader Helen Tynan: "Lots of people chatted the next day about what they had done, and how long the evening had seemed with lots of times for doing things." The idea spread from the People dept to the whole of Google Dublin and has now gone international.

> "Leaders who can't do their jobs in a regular 40-hour work week must be either incredibly unproductive, bad at managing their time, or terrible at delegating."
>
> Alexander Kjerulf, Leading with Happiness

Commute by bicycle not car: It will make you happier and reduce your risk of a heart attack by 24%, and a 20% lower risk of death overall. (Here)

Keep 50% of your time unscheduled: Do you have meetings and activities throughout your day? Where do you have spare time for people? Tom Peters suggests in Extreme Humanism: "every leader should routinely keep a substantial portion of his or her time—I would say as much as 50 percent—unscheduled

Time for Rachel: My PA sets aside "Time for Rachel" in my diary. Rachel Street, CEO, Heart of Kent Hospice.

If Jeff can do it: "I want to tell you a story about a guy called Jeff. Back in 1994, Jeff left the long-hours of a highly paid corporate career on Wall Street to start his own business. But Jeff doesn't like to work too hard. He goes to bed early, gets eight hours' sleep and, after waking up, likes to "putter" a while, enjoying his morning coffee, reading the newspaper, cooking big breakfasts and hanging out with his kids before they go to school. After breakfast, he does the dishes before starting work at 10am.

"Jeff realized a few years ago that he works best in the mornings, so he likes to get any "high IQ" meetings done and dusted before lunchtime. Jeff is well aware that, due to decision fatigue, making good choices gets harder throughout the day so, by 5pm, he'll postpone any decision making until 10am the next day. Try to picture Jeff, and you might think of a relaxed entrepreneur, with plenty of time for his friends and family, perhaps running a lifestyle business or small consultancy. It's unlikely you'll have pictured Jeff Bezos. If Jeff Bezos can make billions and enjoy his life, why are you sacrificing so much?

(From The Hard Work Myth by Barnaby Lashbrooke

Taking time to reflect

If you take 15 minutes to reflect at the end of the day, you can improve your productivity by 22.8%. That's the conclusion of a study at Harvard Business School. Participants spent 15 minutes writing in a journal to embed their learning from the day, and produced these dramatic results.

Walk in the woods with your dog: One headteacher from Hillingdon described to me how every Monday morning – in school time – she goes for a two hour walk in the woods with her dog. "In terms of the thinking I get done, it is the most productive part of my working week".

Mindfulness: For the last year I have been spending just five minutes each morning in mindful reflection. I find giving myself that space makes a real difference to how I feel during the day that follows. Here are five large companies who believe in mindfulness, one of my most popular blogs.

10 days a year at home: Another headteacher, this time from Gloucestershire, told me how they got their governors to agree to them spending 10 days a year, during school term, at home. They would then use this time to think about how to improve processes, ways of working, or develop strategies, for the school.

Morning and afternoon Fika: In Sweden it is standard practice to take a 15 minute break for tea and cakes, normally at 10am and 3pm. "Every company I have worked in has taken Fika twice a day", Annie Hagman

Book in innovation time: One thing we learnt from doing this at Happy was that, if you want innovation and creativity, you have to set aside the time for it. It has to be booked in. So every month our key people on our leadership programmes come together for 3 hours to look at what can be improved. It means our delivery is continually changing and improving.

Break your arm: As I worked with one group of NHS leaders, many described how they had no time in their hectic schedules to reflect. Then one surgeon mentioned that, a couple of years previously, he had broken his arm. For three months he couldn't go in the operating theatre. Instead he used the time to look at their processes and came up with new ways of working that resulted in efficiencies way beyond that three months in benefit. Don't wait to break your arm – can you find the time?

Put people to work on improvement: A partner in a GP surgery in Exeter described how they took over an underperforming surgery. Everybody felt overworked and without any spare time to think about how to improve the service.

"So we worked out who were the most creative people, best able to come up with new approaches. And we deliberately timetabled innovation time for them, even in what felt a very hectic schedule. The core question was 'what are GPs (our most expensive resource) doing that other people could do?". She went on to list a dozen improvements that this had led to, resulting in less pressure and actually improving the service to patients.

Take a break in a café: Most mornings, on my cycle into work, I stop in a café for a hot chocolate. I either spend that time getting some writing done (yep, I'm in a café right now) or taking time to reflect before heading into the busy office. I often stop off on the way home too (though I do have the benefit of a short, 14 minute, commute).

End of day reflection: Or use the Harvard idea, and take 15 minutes at the end of each day to reflect. Apparently the benefit is greatest if you write rather than just think about it, and writing by hand is better than typing it into a computer (this is why leaders on our <u>four-day Happy Workplace Leadership Programme</u> now receive one of our Happy Planner and learning journals for planning and reflection). Try it for a week and see what happens.

The Twitter boss who set aside two hours a day for reflection: One more great example from Kim Scott's book Radical Candour. She describes how Dick Costelo, while CEO of Twitter from 2010 to 2015, would schedule two hours thinking time into his diary – every day. During this time Twitter grew from 30 million monthly active users to over 300 million.

An hour a day to think: Peter Drucker, the world renowned business guru, argued that managers should set aside an hour a day to think.

(Tom Peters, The Excellence Dividend)

Find your desert. "I believe it's important to find a learning space, take time to reflect. Eg, switch off the computer and let your thoughts bubble up." Adele Paterson, International Health Partners:

Set aside time for reflection and development: "We hold two inset weeks at different parts of the year, purely for staff development. It is worth it." Mervyn Kaye: Youth Works

Build in time to reflect: So many of us are so busy we don't find time to be effective. You have to plan reflection time, I suggested. One example is when people banned eating at desks in the Happy office, forcing people to take a break. Another is setting aside three hours every six weeks, to think about what we want to change and improve.

Reflect together at work: At Heiligenfeld, every Tuesday morning, 350 staff come together and engage in joint reflection. "Employees often credit [this] one practice in particular for making the company an outstanding workplace", explains Frederick Laloux.

Four silent days a year: Laloux also describes how, once a quarter, Heiligenfeld holds a mindfulness day which both staff and patients spend in silence. "Patients are invited to remain entirely silent (they wear a tag with the word "silence" to remind each other), while the staff speaks only when needed, in whispers (staff wear a tag with the word "mindfulness")."

(Laloux, Reinventing Organisations)

Clarity Breaks: "We take 30 mins every week to just think about the team/dept/business and how we can improve", Matt Smalley, AccessPlanIT

Performance Reviews are better if you take a holiday: "In the U.S. and Canada … for each 10 vacation hours a person took, we found on average that performance reviews were 8 percent higher," said Maryella Gockel, flexibility strategy leader at EY.

Health & Wellbeing

Make exercise part of the culture: At NextJump all staff are encouraged to go to the gym twice a week, and supported to eat healthily. And the dance battle, above, certainly helps too.

They have a fitness competition where every NextJumper is put into one of 5 Fitness Teams. The team that collectively do exercise the most in any given week, receive a monetary incentive which is split between the team. "We went from 25% of the company working out twice a week to 95%!"

3pm exercise: Every day at 3pm at Happy work stops for staff (or those who want to) to do some stretching and core-building exercises. Started by Nicole Martin, then our newest member of staff, the options are chosen from a hat full of exercise ideas. It has became a very popular break.

Companies that use mindfulness

Search inside yourself at Google: It is possible to say that Chade Meng Tan has revolutionized Google: every year, thousands of employees take his mindfulness course Search Inside Yourself. The waiting time for enrolling in the course is over six months. The huge success of the initiative is clear. Tan has managed to convince the scientists and techies at Google, previously suspicious of "hippie stuff", to completely embrace the practices by explaining the neuroscience behind them.

General Mills finds 89% of their leaders become better listeners after mindfulness: General Mills, the food company behind products such as Old El Paso, Häagen-Dazs and Cheerios, have welcomed the mindfulness revolution and seen their company grow as a result. This is a review of their 7-week mindfulness and meditation program: 83% of participants said they took time every day to optimize their productivity, up 23% from before the course, 80% of senior executives reported that they had improved their decision-making process after the course, and 89% said they had become better listeners. (Gelles, 2013). In 2011, the Leadership Excellence Magazine ranked General Mills the best for developing leaders in 2011, up from 14th in 2010.

Thousands at Intel practice yoga and mindfulness: Intel is a company that battles with stress. Lindsey Van Driel commented: "Across the board, every single person we talk to (at Intel) experiences stress (...) if they weren't stressed it would mean they're not working hard enough" (Intel, 2013). However, inspired by Chade Meng Tan's initiatives at Google, Van Driel decided to do something about it. Today, thousands of Intel employees have participated in the Awake@Intel programme, which includes yoga and mindfulness practices. Similarly to Google, many of the participants were hard-core scientists, initially reporting scepticism towards the benefits of the course. However, after the course the participants reported improved creativity, well-being and focus, decreased levels of stress and stronger enthusiasm in projects and meetings.

$9 million saved in health care costs after yoga and meditation at Aetna: Aetna is a medical insurance company and one of the 100 largest firms in the U.S. by revenue. After a near-fatal accident, 58-year-old CEO Mark T. Bertolini decided to drastically transform his company. His measures included a 33% salary increase for the lowest paid employees, and the establishment of free yoga and meditation classes. These measures have had a huge impact: after the first year, the company reported a whopping $9 million saving in health care costs! Moreover, the employee who participated in the classes reported a 28% decrease in stress levels and an increase in productivity levels. These improvements were estimated to be adding a value of circa $3,000/employee a year (Gelles, 2015)

Even Goldman Sachs is including mindfulness: Perhaps the most surprising name on the list, the investment bank Goldman Sachs is now warming towards mindfulness practices. Although maybe not fully widespread in the firm (yet), the firm does use mindfulness in wellbeing seminars and also promotes the use of the meditation app Headspace. Sally Boyle, head of human capital management at Goldman, comments: "In years to come we'll be talking about mindfulness as we talk about exercise now" (in Agnew, 2014).

Feel restored: "We have been running weekly mindfulness session, online, with a lovely lady. Feel really restored after it.

Most of the team comes to it." Olivia Clymer, CEO, HealthWatch Central West London

Be productive not busy

Don't waste time being busy: When I discussed with Kirsten Regal, one of Sun's leaders, how little their meeting rooms seemed to be used, she quipped, "We don't waste time being busy."' (Laloux)

Stop bragging about overwork: The people who brag about trading sleep for endless slogs and midnight marathons are usually the ones who can't point to actual accomplishments.

> "It doesn't have to be crazy at work", Jason Fried and David Heinemeier Hansson

Monk mode morning. At least 2 or 3 days each week, have no meetings and don't check your Inbox, before 11. Instead get stuff done. With thanks to Bruce Daisley, VP of Twitter (author of The Joy of Work).

Meeting-free hour at lunch time: At Praxis in Bethnal Green no meetings are allowed between 1pm and 2pm. "It helps set boundaries", explains CEO Sally Daglian.

Trust-based leaders don't spend their time in meetings: "When I met Allen Carlson, the CEO of Sun Hydraulics (a publicly listed company), I asked him if he would show me his agenda for the week. He had only four meetings planned in that entire week, two of which were with me", Frederick Laloux (Laloux, Reinventing organisations)

No meetings Wednesdays: "Have no meetings on a Wednesday - no internal or external meetings one day a week" Matt Smalley, AccessPlanIt

> "In almost every situation, the expectation of an immediate response is an unreasonable expectation."
>
> "It doesn't have to be crazy at work", Jason Fried and David Heinemeier Hansson

Customer-Employee Value portal: This portal is for employees to put forward ideas, which customers then read and feedback on - leading directly to improved ideas and improved service. HCL

Reduce meeting time: Go for 25 minutes (instead of 30), 45 minutes (instead of one hour) or 90 minutes (instead of two hours). You are like to find you get as much done, plus you may get the chance to perform the actions you promised to do before the next meeting.

The 20 second rule: "If something is making your life or your customers life 20 seconds harder, stop it." Sarah Metcalfe

> "I would tell my staff about the "dinosaur's tail": As a leader grows more senior, his bulk and tail become huge, but like the brontosaurus, his brain remains modestly small. When plans are changed and the huge beast turns, its tail often thoughtlessly knocks over people and things. That the destruction was unintentional doesn't make it any better." (McChrystal)

Shorter Working Day or Working Week

Toyota, Sweden: 6 hours shifts are more productive than 8 hours: A Toyota mechanic/dealership in Gothenberg has switched from 8 hour shifts to 6 hours. Martin Banck explained the approach at Woohoo's happiness conference in Copenhagen earlier this month. (If your Swedish is good, check out his talk).

There was no fall in production and the change led to happier staff, happier customers and more profits. With both shifts able to be fitted into a daytime, costs fell. Martin did display a slide on the disadvantages of the shorter day. The slide was blank.

Goodman Masson, London: Its Friday, its 3.30 - go home: Goodman Masson is a financial recruitment agency, based in London. A couple of summers ago they decided to stop work at 3.30 on Fridays, enabling staff to enjoy the weather and start the weekend early.

"I analysed all the data", explains CEO Guy Hayward "and it had no effect on the level of sales. We track the phone time of our consultants and this actually went up, as did morale. So we extended it throughout the year. At 3.30pm every Friday I send round an email telling people to go home."

Is it time for a four-day week?

Most people in work feel busy and hectic. Many work long hours. But are we productive? Instead of encouraging long hours working, some organisations are experimenting with getting people to work less: four days instead of five for the same salary. Some are reducing hours by the full 20%, others are increasing the working day on the remaining four days. Check out the companies below.

Economist John Maynard Keynes famously predicted, back in 1930, that we could all be working just 15 hours in the future. In 1926 Henry Ford had introduced the five day 40 hour working week and found that productivity and profits increased. But reductions in the working week have more or less stalled since then.

1. Microsoft Japan: 40% productivity gain

This story went global last week, and for good reasons. The 2,300 employees of Microsoft Japan were given Friday off over the summer and found that cutting working hours by 20% resulted in a 40% increase in productivity. It also led to 25% less absence and 23% less use of electricity with 92% of staff saying they enjoyed the four-day week.

One key step was apparently to cut meetings to 30 minutes. As CEO Takuya Hirano put it, "Work a short time, rest well and learn a lot."

2. Perpetual Guardian: 20% productivity increase

In New Zealand, the finance company Perpetual Guardian moved to a permanent four day week after a two month trial. MD Andrew Barnes comments that "Our total profitability, revenue, service standards didn't drop, so as a consequence our productivity must have gone up 20%."

What did change was a reduction in stress, and improvements in work-life balance, loyalty to the firm and employee empowerment. In this TEDx video Andrew explains how the idea was triggered after reading an Economist study that found that UK workers only worked productively for 2.5 hours a day.

3. IIH Denmark, 3 key steps to productivity

In this 3 minute video, technology company IIH Denmark explain three ways in which they made a four day week work by finding ways to become more productive:

1) Use the Pomodoro method. Time 25-minute work sprints, where you cannot be disturbed

2) Set meetings to 20 or 45 minutes, not half an hour or an hour

3) Decide which work is A (specialist), B (others within the organisation can do) or C (mundane, could be easily outsourced)

4. Synergy Vision: More happiness, less overtime

London based medical PR company Synergy Vision switched to a four day week in September 2019 after a six month trial. They found a big boost in staff happiness (those rating themselves 9 or 10 went from 12% to 51%), the proportion feeling they had a positive work/life balance doubled and less people needed to work overtime.

Synergy is moving from a five-day 40 hour week to a four day 36 hour week. The company ranked 2nd in the 2019 UK Best Workplaces (20 – 50 employees).

5. Memiah: scientific trial

London based Memiah — seeking to build a happier, healthy society — are currently trialling a four day week for six months in a scientific study in partnership with Anglia Ruskin University. Hair samples are being taken and cortisol levels (the body's stress indicator) being measured. Memiah will continue to be open for five days a week and the actual cut in hours is only from 34 to 32.

7. Simply Business: Experimenting with a 30-hour week

Insurance company Simply Business is currently piloting a four day week in its Northampton call centre. It involves switching from a 37.5-hour week in five days to a 30 hour week in four days. Simply Business won the Sunday Times Best Company to Work For in 2016 and CEO Jason Stockwood has written the boot Reboot ("a blueprint for happy, healthy business in the digital age"). The company is currently owned by multibillion-dollar US insurance firm Travelers

8. Femma: A more balanced life

Belgian feminist advocacy organisation Femma are carrying out a one year experiment, which started in January 2019, of a 30 hour week for its 60 staff. They are working with Free University of Brussels researchers to study the impact. Director Eve Brumagne explains: "They have a much more balanced life, new hobbies and are spending more time with their children. People are saying their lives have slowed down."

9. MRL Brighton recruitment consultancy

Brighton-based recruitment firm MRL Consulting Group started a six month trial in April 2019 of a four day working week for its 56 employees across UK, France and Germany. CEO David Stone explains: "I want to give the staff more time to relax, get the life admin done, do whatever it is they need to do when they're not in the office. I want them to have real work-life balance. When people retire, I want them to look back and say MRL was the best place they ever worked."

10. Labour Party: The Skidelsky report

John McDonnell, Labour's Shadow Chancellor, asked economist Lord Skidelsky to produce a report on the possibility of a four day week. Skidelsky argues that working less hours is "good for material and spiritual well-being." While he has been reported as saying that a four-day week was neither "realistic or even desirable," those words were actually used about the idea of capping working hours centrally. Instead he proposes "nudges" to encourage employers towards less hours. Skidelsky argues for encouraging a shorter working week rather than imposing it.

Labour's proposal is for a 32-hour week, which for most companies would be working less days but with slightly longer hours.

11. Normally: four days mean more care in how to create value

Data products studio Normally is now four years into four-day week working. Staff work a standard working day, but for only four days and choose which day they take off. "We've found that by reducing the time we spend at work, we treat the time we do have with more care. It encourages us to be mindful of how we use our time and gets the team to think about the most effective way they can create value." Some useful advice here for others wanting to try it.

12. Pursuit Marketing: 30% boost in productivity

Glasgow based digital marketing Pursuit Marketing has seen a 30% increase in productivity since it adopted a four-day week in 2016. CEO Lorraine Gray says it has resulted in big increases in employee satisfaction and health and led to staff turnover being below 2%. She expects sales to triple to £15 million this year.

13. Radioactive: Better performance, more happiness

PR firm Radioactive adopted a four day week in 2018 and this year reported a strong business performance, high levels of staff happiness, fewer sick days and a spike in recruitment a year after launch. All staff take Fridays off, though they may still communicate with clients by WhatsApp. In return holidays have been reduced by five days and lunch hour cut to 45 minutes.

14. Henley Business School: Two thirds reported increases in productivity

Henley's research, published in a white paper this June called "Four Better Four Worse", suggest that moving to a four day week could save businesses £104 billion a year. They found that 34% of business leaders surveyed, and 46% of those in larger businesses, say making the switch to a four-day working week will be "important for future business success". They suggest that we are likely to see more trials in the coming years.

They state that half of all businesses surveyed have enabled a four-day week for some or all of their staff (though not on the basis of four days' work for five days' pay) and claim that £92 billion in savings have already been made.

Benefits of a four-day week

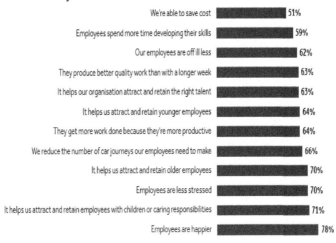

We're able to save cost	51%
Employees spend more time developing their skills	59%
Our employees are off ill less	62%
They produce better quality work than with a longer week	63%
It helps our organisation attract and retain the right talent	63%
It helps us attract and retain younger employees	64%
They get more work done because they're more productive	64%
We reduce the number of car journeys our employees need to make	66%
It helps us attract and retain older employees	70%
Employees are less stressed	70%
It helps us attract and retain employees with children or caring responsibilities	71%
Employees are happier	78%

15. Four-day weeks in US schools: one hour longer on the day

Schools across 21 states are apparently experimenting with a three-day weekend, with an extra hour on the remaining days. Some see this as controversial. It seems that some have seen benefits and continued four day working, while others have switched back to five days.

16. Happy: Pilot for a month

Here at Happy we decided to pilot a four-day week for a month, in August. The results were interesting. Over half our people felt they got as much done in four days as they previously did in five. However some did find it increased their stress. We have agreed to extend to two months next year. More here.

Could you try a four-day week for a month?

Switching completely to a four-day week feels very daunting. However most companies start with a trial, of maybe one month. Could your organisation do that? Apparently 63% of Britons support a four day week, more than in any of the six other European nations surveyed.

17. Case Study: WL Gore

> "My friends at Fast Company had labeled it as the world's most innovative company, so I thought I should learn more. That first visit was weird, even disconcerting. I found virtually nothing at Gore that matched up with the management practices I had observed in hundreds of other companies—no titles, no bosses and no formal hierarchy.
>
> "I felt like a surgeon who had opened up a patient who looked human, but turned out to be filled with wires and circuits. Yet as I got to know Gore, I realized I had this analogy backwards. Gore was *deeply* human and by contrast, all those other companies I had studied were cyborgs. Gore's management model seemed wacky only because I had grown accustomed to the inhuman practices that predominated in most other companies."
>
> Professor Hamel, Wall Street Journal, 18/3/2000

WL Gore has been in the Fortune 100 best workplaces list from 1984 to now, one of very few companies to have been placed every year. It has been practising a freedom based approach for over 50 years.

They are best known as the makers of Goretex, though they have 1,000 products including a wide range of life saving medical devices. In 2018 they had 9,500 employees and $3.5 billion in sales worldwide and have regularly been rated as one of the most innovative companies on the planet.

Douglas MacGregor

The enterprise (a word they use instead of company) was set up in 1958 by Bill and Vieve Gore. Bill Gore was heavily influenced by Douglas MacGregor's The Human Side of Management, which posed two management approaches: Theory X (where workers are not trusted) and Theory Y, (where they are).

At the time MacGregor said that he'd never actually visited a company that was genuinely based on Theory Y. You could argue that Bill set out to prove that Theory Y could work and built his company on the basis of complete trust

From the early days the focus was on applying technology to have a meaningful impact on society. Bill Gore wanted to support human fulfilment, embodied in a set of principles and management practices designed to foster trust, initiative and enable the emergence of natural leaders.

WL Gore describes itself as an "enterprise" and has leaders, not bosses. The nearest equivalent of a manager is a Champion, who the associate chooses. There are no job descriptions. Instead each associate sets down their commitment for the year, a commitment that is regarded very seriously.

Bureaucracy is kept to a minimum. Teams are self-organising, with generally around 8-10 people. "You get bigger than that, it's not a small team, it's a bigger team, then you've got other problems." (John Housego)

One key saying at Gore is "if you want to be a leader, you'd better find some followers", because you won't get appointed from above. At the 2016 Happy Workplace conference John Housego explained how he had come to run the UK manufacturing plant. "I'd been there three years when the plant manager called me into his office and said 'John, I'm off to the States for nine months, I've asked the team, they want you to lead the plant.'" John thought he lacked the experience. The response: "Well the team think you can, and that's all that matters."

Even the appointment of the new CEO is a group decision, with the opinions of dozens of staff members being sought.

Key Factors for a Happy Workplace

John went on to explain the key factors that he felt make WL Gore a happy workplace:

1. Clarity of commitment that's written by you.
2. Ability to use your strengths – so, you're in your sweet spot.
3. Rewards decided by your peers – so the team that you respect and you work for and you help deliver things judge whether you've done a good job or not.
4. Working in teams that know and trust each other; hopefully you've got a good friend that's in there.
5. And most importantly, a voice that is heard. If you don't have a voice, what are you in the meeting for? Why don't you just read the meeting notes? If it's a communication of "this is what it's going to be" then just get the dictum afterwards. If you're in a meeting, I'm expecting a voice. I want to know your opinion.

Its guiding principles include Commitment ("We are not assigned tasks; rather, we each make our own commitments and keep them") and Waterline ("Everyone at Gore consults with other knowledgeable Associates before taking actions that might be 'below the waterline,' causing serious damage to the enterprise").

In Gore's "lattice organisation", anyone can talk to anyone, and no one tells another what to do. "If you tell anybody what to do here, they'll never work for you again," one associate told Prof Hamel

Gore has a disarmingly simple working definition of leadership: a capability to attract followers, for which no other qualifications are a substitute.

WL Gore is quite secretive, regarding its culture as a competitive advantage. I know of no book written about it. Articles include this (2008) and this (2019) from the Financial Times and this piece in the Wall Street Journal from Gary Hamel. And this speech from John Housego at the 2016 Happy Workplaces conference.

18. Select managers who are good at managing

Too often Managers are chosen because of their core skills or length of service, rather than their potential for bringing the most out of people. Make sure your people are supported by somebody who is good at doing that, and find other routes for those whose strengths lie elsewhere. Even better, allow people to choose their own managers.

> 70% of the variance in team engagement is determined solely by the manager. It's the manager.
>
> Jim Clifton, Jim Harter, Gallup (It's the Manager)

Less than a third of people have the potential to be great managers: Gallup believes that only one in ten people have the right talents to be a great manager and another 20% can get there with the right coaching and development. They suggest you should forget the rest – in terms of management roles. Gallup believes that only 18% of current managers have the talent to do the role. *State of the American Manager*

Are you a multiplier of your people's talent? "Do you act as the expert, setting strategy, making key decisions and protecting your people? Those are diminishing behaviours. Or do you search out the talent in your people, create debate and step out of the way – to become a multiplier?" (Liz Wiseman, Multipliers)

> "Excellence is learning the names and school year of all 14 of your team members' kids." Tom Peters, Extreme Humanism

Find the right people to be managers and increase revenues by 27%: That is the verdict of Gallup's 2015 *State of the American Manager* report. The best managers, they argue, "are gifted with the ability to inspire employees, drive outcomes, overcome adversity, hold people accountable, build strong relationships and make tough decisions based on performance rather than politics".

> "When Gallup asked thousands of managers how they became managers, the top two reasons they gave were: success in a prior nonmanagement role and tenure." Jim Clifton, Jim Harper, Gallup, (It's the Manager)

The role of the manager

> "I see 99% of my job as getting out of the way. Help set the direction, give assurance and then get out of the way" Alison Sturgess-Durdon, Director, Mayden

Google gives their managers lots of people to manage: At some companies there is an upper limit to how many people report to one manager. Eric Schmidt (then Google CEO) made clear that Google suggests a minimum of seven and that at one point the Head of Engineering had 130 direct reports.

"With that many direct reports—most managers have a lot more than seven—there simply isn't time to micromanage." (Eric Schmidt "How Google Works")

One coach per 400 staff: At Buurtzorg, nurses work in self-managing teams of ten to twelve. Separately there are coaches that can be called in for support but only about one for every 400 people in the company. "It's deliberate", explained founder Jos de Blok to me at the 2019 Thinkers50 conference. "Spread among that many people there is no danger they will start doing manager-like things."

Calm the Fish: To get great pictures, an underwater photographer must make sure they don't disturb the fish with their presence.

"As a manager you need to aim for the same thing. When, that when you walk around your presence makes no difference – people behave as they would when you are not there." Donna Reeves

Business is about people not numbers. "Throw away your reports and your KPIs", explains founder John Timpson of Timpsons, "and get out and talk to the people in your company. Business success is all about the people and making them feel valued"

> "Here is my radical proposition: a business leader's job is to create great teams that do amazing work on time. That's it. That's the job of management."
>
> Patty McCord, Chief Talent Officer, Netflix (in Powerful)

The manager's role is to stay out of the way: "Google is famously viewed as a bottom-up company, one that empowers even very young employees to drive decision-making. The managers' role is mostly to stay out of the way, sometimes to help, but never to interfere too much." (Kim Scott, Radical Candour)

Listen and seek to understand: "At Apple, as at Google, a boss's ability to achieve results had a lot more to do with listening and seeking to understand than it did with telling people what to do; more to do with debating than directing; more to do with pushing people to decide than with being the decider; more to do with persuading than with giving orders; more to do with learning than with knowing." (Kim Scott, Radical Candour)

Give the quiet ones a voice: Jony Ive, Apple's chief design officer, once said at an Apple University class that a manager's most important role is to "give the quiet ones a voice." (Kim Scott, Radical Candour)

> "Enable your people to use their full potential, not just 60% (or less) of it. It's not about you as a manager. It's about the team. If you trust the team, they will show up."
>
> Donna Reeves, ex-Director, Kingfisher plc

No managers but there are leaders: At Nearsoft, a Mexican outsourcing company, they have never had managers. "We don't have bosses but we do have leaders", explained Anabal Montiel, "They emerge organically and last as long as needed. People do take ownership of certain processes." So who holds people to account?

"The team. If somebody isn't performing, the team intervenes. There's a lot of peer pressure to do a good job. You are accountable to a lot of people. Having freedom doesn't mean you can do whatever you want. It means there is not one person following you and making sure you do what you have to do. Instead we have an awful lot of feedback processes."

Talk less, listen more: Multipliers talk 10% or less of the time at team meetings, diminishers are likely to talk 30% or more. (From Liz Wiseman, Multipliers)

Be prepared to say "I don't know": For Adele Paterson of IHP, this gives the chance for somebody else to step up

Day on the shop floor: "Spend a day in uniform (or equivalent...). Regularly spend a day on the shop floor, working with front-line staff." Rachel Street, CEO, Heart of Kent Hospice

> "The role of the director is to create a space where the actors and actresses can become more than they have ever been before, more than they've dreamed of being."

Listen

"My education in leadership began in Washington when I was an assistant to Defense Secretary William Perry. He was universally loved and admired by heads of state . . . and our own and allied troops. A lot of that was because of the way he listened. Each person who talked to him had his complete, undivided attention. Everyone blossomed in his presence, because he was so respectful, and I realized I wanted to affect people the same way." Tom Peters, Extreme Humanism.

Think like a 3-year-old: "Instead of thinking you know the answers, regain the curiosity of a 3 year old. Wonder why and wonder why not. Ask lots of questions." Cathy Busani, MD, Happy

Courageous conversations

Apple's Chief Design Officer Jony Ive told a story about a time when he pulled his punches when criticizing his team's work. When Steve Jobs asked Jony why he hadn't been clearer about what was wrong, Jony replied, "Because I care about the team." To which Steve replied, "No, Jony, you're just really vain. You just want people to like you." Recounting the story, Jony said, "I was terribly cross because I knew he was right." Kim Scott, Radical Candour

Feedback

"Almost half (47%) of employees report that they received feedback from their manager "a few times or less" in the past year. What's more, only 26% of employees strongly agree that the

Beyond 360 Degree Evaluation: Most big companies now get
managers to be evaluated by peers and by some of those they
manage. HCL's innovation was to open this up, so you could
evaluate anybody in the company that you came into contact
with. As well as the widespread feedback, the unexpected result
was that managers began to be judged by how many responses
they received. It became a measure of their circle of influence.
(Vineet Nayar, Employees First, Customers Second)

Two Tracks of Management

"The best organizations believe that not everyone should be a
manager, and they create high-value career paths for individual
contributor roles. No one should feel like their progress depends
on getting promoted to manager." Jim Clifton, Jim Harper, Gallup
(It's the Manager)

Create "Dual career tracks": Hay Group explains DCT's: "the
defining attribute of a dual career track is that, at some point in
the path, the individual is presented with a choice" (2004, p.4).
Employees get to choose between a managerial career, or one of
expertise which does not involve people responsibilities. Although
the concept of DCT's has existed for decades, this practice has
mostly been used by a handful of world-leading technology and
science companies.

Cougar created a judo belt system for reward: Happy was
training engineers from software company Cougar in
management skills. At the end of the day, several managers
approached the facilitator and said "this isn't really for us. We're
going to approach our MD and ask if we can stop being
managers".

Clive Hutchinson, Cougar's Managing Director, turned out to be open to this. The company created a second career path for those who wanted to remain engineers, based around the Judo belt system. Engineers would start as a light blue belt, move up through white and brown to the ultimate black belt. It has proved highly successful as an alternative career path.

Mastercard have special career paths for people who want to progress but not manage people: Employees can either progress as consultants (functional) or leaders (managerial). They have these paths in project management and sales and plan to implement them in product development, marketing and communications. In 2013, Forbes named Mastercard one of the 50 Best Companies to Work For.

Kraft Foods have used dual tracks since 1995: At Kraft Foods Inc. in the U.S, they introduced DCL's back in 1995. The implementations were hugely successful, and only four years later the company reported a decrease in employee turnover from 9% down to 6% (Cole-Gomolski, 1999).

The post-it would not exist without dual tracks: One of the most tangible results of a dual career track system is the existence of the Post-it. Arthur Fry at 3M was responsible for developing the best-selling product. According to Fry, the Post-it would not have existed today if 3M's dual career paths had not been in place. Fry admitted that one of the reasons behind his choice to remain in the field, and not pursue a managerial career, was because of the possibility of becoming one of their highly regarded "corporate scientists" (Tomasko, 1995).

Triple career tracks at BP: Another company that has reported the success of their dual careers system is BP. In fact, they even have a triple career system; functional specialists, functional leaders and business leaders. Thus, they differentiate between functional managers and general managers. They do however encourage moving between the categories.

Triple tracks again at Rolls-Royce: At Rolls-Royce, they pursue a similar approach to that of BP. There are three types of manager - Specialist roles (functional), Technical Manager (functional) and Project Manager (traditional). Rolls Royce have received praise for the internal structures and are consistently in the top 25 best companies to work for in the UK.

Apple would never have existed without Woz being allowed a separate role: You will know that Apple was founded by Steve Jobs and Steve Wozniak. But do you know the difficulty Steve Jobs had getting Woz to leave Hewlett Packard to set up Apple? He explained that he would no longer be a small cog, but would manage a whole team of engineers. Woz said no, he reckoned he'd stay at HP. Jobs kept trying to persuade him, emphasising his importance and how many people he'd be in charge of.

Then Apple investor Mike Markulla took Steve Jobs aside and explained that Woz just wanted to be an engineer. He didn't want to be responsible for other people. Jobs changed his approach: he offered Woz great kit, all the resources he needed and promised "Woz, you will never have to manager anybody." That sounded good to Woz and he made the move. The rest is history.

The Individual Contributor at Google: Google's engineering teams solved this problem by creating an "individual contributor" career path that is more prestigious than the manager path and sidesteps management entirely. This has been great for the growth of these engineers; it's also good for the people whom they would otherwise have been managing. When people become bosses just to "get ahead" rather than because they want to do what bosses do, they perform, at best, a perfunctory job and often become bosses from hell. (Kim Scott, Radical Candour)

The role is to coach

Imagine instead that you have a manager who genuinely cares about you and wants you to be the best you can be. A manager who builds your confidence, who challenges you but also provides support – even when you get stuff wrong. A manager who asks you questions, rather than tells, and helps you find your own solutions.

Might you actually look forward to seeing your manager?

"Today's employees want a coach, not a boss. Moving your managers from boss to coach not only increases employee engagement and improves performance, but it's also essential to changing your culture." Jim Clifton, Jim Harter, Gallup (It's the Manager)

Managers are there to support at Timpsons. Founder John Timpson: "Our managers are not allowed to tell anybody what to do. Their key role is to listen". They are also expected to know their people. One test of managers is whether they can name the children of the people they manage.

The most important behaviour of managers is to be a good coach: Google researched what were the most effective behaviours of managers, based on analysis of tens of thousands of performance reviews. They came up with 8 positive behaviours. The top three were:

1. Be a Good Coach
2. Empower your people, don't micro-manage
3. Show interest in your people

"Project Oxygen initially set out to prove that managers don't matter and ended up demonstrating that good managers were crucial."

Weekly one-to-ones at Innocent: At Innocent that coaching role is seen as so important that every member of staff is expected to have a weekly one-to-one session with their manager. Their office has been designed to have lots of small private rooms for those sessions.

No managers, just coaches at Buurtzorg: "At Buurtzorg, there is no managerial ladder to climb; coaches are selected for their coaching capacity—they tend to be older, highly experienced nurses with strong interpersonal skills. The span of support (what in traditional organizations would be called "span of control") of Buurtzorg's regional coaches is broad; on average, a coach supports 40 to 50 teams."

"Coaches shouldn't have too much time on their hands, or they risk getting too involved with teams, and that would hurt teams' autonomy. Now they take care of only the most important questions. We gave some of the first teams from Buurtzorg quite intensive support and attention, and today we still see that they are more dependent and less autonomous than other teams." Jos de Blok (Laloux)

> "I still get to do the 'people' stuff I loved as a manager, it's just that now I use a whole range of different techniques to support colleagues to find their own solutions, and run with their own ideas. It's liberating." Alison Sturgess-Durdon, Director, Mayden

Let people choose their managers

For many people it is their manager who makes them unhappy at work. A CMI (Chartered Marketing Institute) survey found that

49% would take a pay cut if they were able to change their manager.

So why don't we let people choose a different manager? It may not make sense in a traditional hierarchical organisation but in a more flexible workplace, especially where the role of the manager is to coach, why would you not let people choose their managers?

Choose your manager at WL Gore: At Gore, makers of Gore-tex, you can choose anybody to play that role. They have a saying "if you want to be a leader, you'd better find some followers"

Over 20 years of choosing your manager at Happy: At Happy people have been able to choose their manager since 2000. As we have moved towards becoming a self-managing organisation, this choice has switched to choosing your coach.

Choose your counsellor at EY: At most management consultancies employees are engaged on projects for months or years. Yet the person who manages the project is rarely their actual manager.

At EY they have a counsellor. "The role is to create degree of consistency, take care of their career, their development, the pastoral aspect," explains Amanda Gethin, Head of HR.

One friend at EY told me they were on the verge of leaving at the end of their first year, because they didn't get on with their counsellor. Then a colleague told them they could change their counsellor. They did so and have gone on to thrive.

Choosing managers in the public sector: At one public sector organisation in the West Country a department of 600 people lets people choose their manager. There is a spreadsheet, where each manager spells out how many people they would like to manage and what they feel they can contribute.

One individual told me that they had chosen three different managers over five years, not because they had difficulties but because they saw different needs. "I now feel like I am in charge of my career progression."

Choose your team at DreamHost: At the Los Angeles based web hosting provider, after a reorganisation, followed a practice of "choose your favourite product to work on", and let people choose their own team – rather than being allocated one. They say this resulted in greater efficiency and increased performance from giving team members a choice. (Worldblu, 50 transformational practices)

Choose another team at any time: "At FAVI, a simple but powerful relief valve exists, should a team leader find the taste of power too sweet: workers can choose at any moment to join another team", explains Frederick Laloux (Laloux)

> "Your title makes you a manager. Your people make you a leader."
>
> Debbie Biondolillo, Apple's former head of human resources,
>
> (from Eric Schmidt, How Google Works)

Not everybody wants to be a manager: Apple was founded by Steve Jobs and Steve Wozniak, known as Woz. For Mike Markulla, the initial investor, a condition of that investment was that both Steves were on board as full-time employees of Apple.

So Steve Jobs went to Woz and explained that he would no longer be a small cog, but would manage a whole team of engineers. Woz said no, he reckoned he'd stay at HP. Jobs kept trying to persuade him, emphasising his importance and how many people he'd be in charge of.

But Mike Markulla actually understood something that Jobs did not. He took Steve Jobs aside and explained that Woz just wanted to be an engineer. He didn't want to be responsible for other people.

Jobs changed his approach: he offered Woz great kit, all the resources he needed and promised "Woz, you will never have to manager anybody." That sounded good to Woz and he made the move. The rest is history.

Rotating Leadership

Rotating leadership at Orpheus Chamber Orchestra: At this Grammy award winning orchestra there is no conductor and leadership roles are rotated amongst orchestra members – establishing fairness and dignity for all the musicians. (Worldblu, 50 transformational practices)

Feedback on Managers

All staff evaluate the CEO: At the DaVita medical group, all of the 74,500 employees are asked to rate the CEO, Kent Thiry, on how well he is living DaVita's seven core values. His scores are presented on stage in front of 3,000 managers at their annual national conference. (WorldBlu, 50 Transformation Practices)

Electing leadership

Elect your leaders at AIESEC: At the "world's largest youth-run organisation", present in more than 180 countries), the international leadership team is elected every year – and has been for over 60 years. (Worldblu, 50 transformational practices)

> "Leaders inspire you to want to go there. Managers help you to get there."
>
> Martin Baker

19. Case Study: Basecamp

Basecamp is a software company, producing the project management tool called, you guessed it, Basecamp. However it doesn't act like most software companies, or indeed like most companies.

Instead of offering benefits to keep people in the office, like free food and laundry, they offer "not a single benefit that would make someone prefer to be at work rather than at home. Not a single benefit that puts work ahead of life." One example is that they pay for the cost of their employee's' vacations.

Instead of encouraging long hours, they discourage them: "Working 40 hours a week is plenty. Plenty of time to do great work, plenty of time to be competitive, plenty of time to get the important stuff done. So that's how long we work at Basecamp. No more. Less is often fine, too. During the summer (which, for Basecamp, is five months, from May to September) we even take Fridays off and still get plenty of good stuff done in just 32 hours."

Instead of aiming to grow, they aim to "stay as small as we can for as long as we can".

Doing nothing is an option

"Doing nothing isn't an option" is a common business phrase. Their response: "Oh, yes, it is. And it's often the best one."

"Rather than continue to invent new products, take on more responsibilities, and grow more obligations, we continually aim to pare down and lighten the load—even when times are great. Cutting back when times are great is the luxury of a calm, profitable, and independent company. "

As leaders they try to hold back: "It takes great restraint as the leader of an organization not to keep lobbing ideas at everyone else. Every such idea is a pebble that's going to cause ripples when it hits the surface. Throw enough pebbles in the pond and the overall picture becomes as clear as mud."

> "If you can't fit everything you want to do within 40 hours per week, you need to get better at picking what to do, not work longer hours. Most of what we think we have to do, we don't have to do at all. It's a choice, and often it's a poor one."

Effectiveness not busyness

"We don't believe in busyness at Basecamp. We believe in effectiveness. How little can we do? How much can we cut out? Instead of adding to-dos, we add to-don'ts.... The only way to get more done is to have less to do."

New ideas are rarely implemented immediately: Instead of "jumping on every new idea right away, we make every idea wait a while. Generally a few weeks, at least."

Rather than put endless effort into every detail, they put lots of effort into separating what really matters from what sort of matters from what doesn't matter at all: "The act of separation should be your highest-quality endeavour. It's easy to say, "Everything has to be great," but anyone can do that. The challenge lies in figuring out where you can be just kinda okay or even downright weak."

Basecamp tries to create an atmosphere where it's easy to get stuff done. Instead of encouraging people to be available at all times, they publish "office hours", the times when subject matter experts are available.

"Taking someone's time should be a pain in the ass. Taking many people's time should be so cumbersome that most people won't even bother to try it unless it's REALLY IMPORTANT! Meetings should be a last resort, especially big ones."

"Most people should miss out on most things most of the time. That's what we try to encourage at Basecamp. JOMO! The joy of missing out. "

They aim not to throw more people at problems. Instead "we chop problems down until they can be carried across the finish line by teams of three."

"Any conversation with more than three people is typically a conversation with too many people. "

At Basecamp the front-line staff make the key decisions: "And who makes the decision about what stays and what goes in a fixed period of time? The team that's working on it. Not the CEO, not the CTO. The team that's doing the work has control over the work. They wield the "scope hammer," as we call it."

"Choose calm"

This case study is taken from "It doesn't have to be crazy at work", Jason Fried and David Heinemeier Hansson, 2018

20. Play to your strengths

Focus on strengths and double your engagement: Gallup has found clear correlations between a managerial focus on employees' strengths (as compared to strengths and weaknesses or only weaknesses) and employee engagement: 67% of the respondents who said that their manager used a strengths-based approach were engaged at work, compared to 30% overall. *State of the American Manager*

> "Only 21% of employees strongly agree that their organization is committed to building the strengths of each employee." Jim Clifton, Jim Harper Gallup (It's the Manager)

Delegate to teams not individuals: Often managers have one or more go-to people that they like to delegate to. At Happy we decided to stop delegating to individuals. Instead we delegate to the team and they decide who is best placed to do a task, whose strength it plays to.

Enable people to play to their strengths: At Happy, Cathy Busani (MD) explained, all staff have used Strengthfinder to understand their strengths. "I facilitate sessions where we look at everybody's jobs and people choose to change what they do to better fit what they like doing and what they are good at."

Find joy in 80% of your work

The aim at Happy is for all staff to find joy in at least 80% of their work. Generally, this means people working to their strengths and doing what they are good at. If it doesn't give them joy, everyone is encouraged to find a different way of doing it or find somebody in the team for whom it does give joy. Everybody estimates their level of joy in the quarterly check-ins. The latest check-ins give an average of 72%, slightly reduced due to a tricky IT system installation going on.

Don't delegate to individuals: At Happy we always delegate to the team and let them work out who wants to do it, whose strength it works to.

Build a team where each person does what they are good at: Neuroscientist and academic Stephen Kosslyn once gave a talk in which he described how people who work together on a team become like "mental prostheses" for each other. What one person doesn't enjoy and isn't good at is what another person loves and excels at. Together, they are "better, stronger, faster." Kim Scott, Radical Candour

Find your strengths: "What, last week, did you look forward to, helped you stay inquisitive, and left you feeling magnificent? That is where to find your strengths." Cathy Busani, MD, Happy (from Marcus Buckingham)

Throw away the job descriptions: Instead of sticking to job descriptions, try throwing the jobs in the air. Ask what people love doing, and they are good at. And switch the roles

Get rid of individual job descriptions: "We moved from individual job descriptions to team descriptions. We agree what the team needs to do and then let the individuals figure out who does what." Cathy Busani

---

"Every minute you spend with somebody who does great work pays off in the team's results much more than time spent with somebody who's failing." Kim Scott, Radical Candour

---

21. Case Study: Reddico

A journey into a self-managing organisation

Inspired by The Happy Manifesto, Reddico started the move to becoming self-managing in March 2018. In just 18 months it has resulted in happier employees, more satisfied customers, higher revenue and a big increase in profits.

They have moved away from having line managers and instead provide their people with coaches. "To be a coach we insisted you went on the Level 5 leadership programme at Happy", explains Head of Operations Luke Kyte.

It is a twenty month programme, including one a day a month in the classroom. 90% of the cost is paid by the government, so it only cost Reddico £900 per person for almost two years of personal development.

"It's great", continues Luke. "It's really interesting how much you can learn, new skills, new ways of communicating. I have really enjoyed self-awareness and increasing awareness of others - understanding how different people can react to different circumstances. It has made a real difference"

Making the Change

"Back in 2017 we thought we had got the culture right. We had free food, a beer fridge, a table tennis table, x box, all the things we thought you needed for a happy workplace."

"We did the Employee Net Promoter Score (NPS) and thought we would get 'World Class'. In fact we got just Good, with some people scoring as passives or detractors. At first I took it quite personally. We were giving all this for free, it seemed ungrateful. Then you start to look at it and think it must be us, must be something going on internally."

"We realised it's not how much you give people for free but how you can free people to give more."

"We looked around and started to get inspiration from books like The Happy Manifesto and Maverick. We talked to the team, to get insight of what they wanted."

"Before it was a bit erratic. One person might ask their line manager if they could work from home and get it. Another might not and ask why not? There was confusion and frustration."

"Now we focus on how people can do what they need to get the job done. Instead of having people work 9-5, controlling the input, we focus on the output. It has been a massive change. Some people work best in morning, some in afternoon, some in evening, why do we pigeonhole people?"

"We started with our own manifesto, 6,000 words long. As in The Happy Manifesto, it came round to values of trust, believing the best in people, giving people that power to do the job in the way they wanted to."

"Then we put the red flags in place: targets (which staff set themselves), NPS, quarterly 360 review – so if something went wrong, we would know about it. To be honest, I looked at it and didn't know if it would work. How can we give all this freedom, surely something will go wrong?"

Reddico is a software development and digital marketing company, employing 24 people on a farm near Tonbridge in Kent.

As much holiday as you want

"They now all work whatever pattern they like and take as much holiday as they want. Though we have a set a minimum of twenty days."

Do people actually take lots of holiday? "Well I've taken 30 days already this year and its only August."

"Not having managers was the bit I was most confused about. Who is responsible for reviews, salary setting, I wondered. But we moved from managers to having two separate roles: department leads are responsible for growing the department and setting strategy. Coaches support and empower people and everybody picks their own coach. Salaries are now decided by a panel elected by the staff."

2018 was the best year so far for the company for revenue. However in 2019 Reddico has increased revenue and profit every month. "And not just by a small amount. In May it was something like a 130% increase in profit."

World Class ENPS

The Employee NPS is now 95, a phenomenal figure. I know of only one other company at that level. The client NPS – measuring client satisfaction - has also gone up, from around 60 to 80.

"What's the secret? We don't have a hard set of rules in place. We just give freedom and trust and responsibility. We say 'This is how we do it, go ahead and show us you can. Just don't have a negative impact on the team with what you are doing."

"The Happy Manifesto was a massive part of it. All the principles behind the Happy Manifesto, we drew as inspiration for our own manifesto. The beliefs, that shift from being a traditional hierarchical business to giving more trust for the team."

Salaries: first panel, picked by the panel. Vote, and the top 4 got picked.

What tips does Luke have for others embarking on the journey to a trust-based workplace? "Believe in it. Go for it. Take it in small manageable steps. Have plan for what you are trying to do. Break down into what will make biggest impact first."

"It took us 9 months to fully roll it out. I had to be freed up to do it. I needed to be solely responsible. You have to have someone dedicated to doing it. Otherwise it gets talked about and promised, but will not happen."

Has anything gone wrong in the transition? "No, not that I can think of."

Are you ready to create a self-managing organisation? Are you ready to give your people the trust and freedom to do a great job?

22. Self Managing Organisations

"How many of you have managers?" asked Alison Sturgess-Durden at the 2019 Happy Workplaces Conference. Lots of hands were raised. "How many of you feel you need to be managed?" she continued. Nobody raised their hand.

Alison, a Director at the software company Mayden, asked why we assume that people need to be "managed" at work. Mayden is one of a growing band of companies that have no managers.

This is one of the big developments since the publication of The Happy Manifesto. There were some self-managing companies at the time. Gary Hamel had just written his article for Harvard Business Review, entitled "First, let's fire all the managers" and based on the US tomato processing company Morning Star.

Companies like WL Gore and Semco also had elements of self management. However the idea really came to prominence when Frederick Laloux published Reinventing Organisations in 2016. This used the term Teal to describe the future of organisations, based on self-managing. He included a dozen such companies.

Some examples of organisations that have no managers:

1) Mayden: Mayden, based in Bath in the UK, switched to a flat structure where "everyone would have an equal say in the life and direction of the company." Instead of managers there are 'volunteer internal peer coaches' who support their colleagues and help them find their own solutions.

2) Buurtzorg: A community care social enterprise in the Netherlands, Buurtzorg has grown from four nurses in 2008 to over 14,000 today. They have no managers, organising instead of teams of 10 to 12 who decide for themselves how to serve their patients. They are said to have saved the Dutch health system billions of euros, deliver outstanding patient care and have been rated the best place to work in the country. More here.

3) Local Cornerstone: Inspired by Buurtzorg, Local Cornerstone — a provider that is transforming the social care sector in Scotland — moved in 2016 to a self-managing approach. "A new flat structure and the removal of managerial roles allows colleagues to genuinely be trusted and empowered to make their own decisions including for example rota management, assigning team member responsibilities, deciding on their own training, peer appraisal and being as creative and innovative as they wish. Our team of coaches are always on hand to provide advice if required."

4) Reddico: Reddico is a digital agency based in Tonbridge in Kent. Head of Operations Luke Kyte explains the philosophy here: "No hours. No managers. Rules set by the team. Let's see what happens next."

5) u2i: u2i is a web technology consulting company based in Krakow in Poland (though with a Head Office in New York). Employing around 60 people, it is renowned for being largely self-managing and for the fact that it distributes fully 100% of its profits in bonuses to employees. Instead of managers they have "Sherpas" to coach and guide. More here.

6) Zappos: US online shoe delivery company Zappos has long been an inspiration. Founder Tony Hsieh outlined his belief in creating a happy working environment in his best seller Delivering Happiness. In 2014 they adopted the Holacracy idea of "management without managers."

7) Valve: Valve is a 400-strong games software company, whose value has been estimated at over $1 billion. It has been manager-free since it was founded in 1996. Check out its brilliant Employee Handbook. Of Managing Director Gabe Newall, it says "of all the people in the company who are not your boss, Gabe is the MOST not your boss." It also includes a remarkably honest "What Valve is not good at" section.

As its website says: "When you give smart talented people the freedom to create without fear of failure, amazing things happen." Unusually it puts its approach down to the political theory of anarcho-syndicalism.

Valve accomplishes all this with a highly unconventional approach to authority. It simply lets its employees decide what to work on. No bosses. No reporting. No oversight. Just "vote with your feet" by choosing projects and tasks that you think are worth your time.

8) Basecamp: A software company that has been around for almost 20 years, Basecamp is known for the remarkable usability of its products. As Inc puts it: "Instead of managers, the company looks for people who can direct their own work and actually produce something, rather than watch others produce."

See the excellent book **It Doesn't Have to be Crazy at Work** by founders Jason Fried and David Heinemeier Hansson for a truly sensible approach to running an organisation.

9) Morning Star: Morning Star, a $700 million tomato processing company, has no managers: "By making the mission the boss and truly empowering people, the company creates an environment where people can manage themselves."

10) WL Gore: Sponsors not bosses. Gore is a multi-billion dollar company with 10,000 staff, once rated the most innovative in the US, and best known for its Goretex product. I have often described Gore as a company where people choose their managers. However their website makes clear that the people they are choosing are "sponsors (not bosses)." There are "no chains of command" and instead associates communicate directly with each other.

11) Treehouse: Founder of Treehouse, Ryan Carson, explains here the decision to do away with managers in June 2013, because the system took people away from doing stuff to structuring. Remove the managers, he argues, and you get so much time back for everyone.

12) Github: A coding company with around 40 employees, one explains: "We do things differently at GitHub: we work out of chat rooms, we don't enforce hours, and we have zero managers. People work on what they want to work on. Product development is driven by whoever wants to drive product."

13) Medium: Jason Stirman explains how he discovered as a manager at Twitter that asking "'What's going on in your life?' was far more effective than asking 'What's blocking you at work?'" At Medium, they have adopted Holacracy.

14) North West Care Cooperative (UK): A small, emerging, CQC Registered co-operative provider of care, or as we prefer to think of it as a "community" whose "users", "employees" (a la Buurtzorg) and "supporting" members care "about" each other. Learn more on their Twitter, @NWCareCoop.

15) Cocoon: Italian-based, though now present across four countries, Cocoon uses an open governance framework that they have called a Liquid Organisation. Read all about it here.

16) Semco: The Brazilian-based manufacturing company was the inspiration for many of us when Ricardo Semler published Maverick in 1992. Read his classic blog, Managing Without Managers, written back in 1989.

In "First, let's fire all the managers", Gary Hamel argued that "a hierarchy of managers exacts a hefty tax on any organisation." A centrally planned approach works no better within an organisation than it did in the Eastern European economies, and is a huge waste of time, money and resources.

At Happy we don't have managers either. We have what we call 'M&Ms' (Mentors and Multipliers), though they could be described as coaches. They help and support our people to work out how to work at their best. (This may be old fashioned compared to some of the companies above, but we do believe our people benefit from having somebody to guide and support them.)

So think about it. Do your managers enhance your work and enable your people? If so, great! Or do they take up huge amount of time and resources doing that management thing?

(Remember that 49% of UK employees, according to a CMI survey, so dislike their manager that they would take a pay cut to be managed by somebody else.)

There is another way. Perhaps it's time for more organisations to try doing away with managers?

23. Companies that reflect these principles

The aim here is to include a list of all the companies that could be said to be self-managing or based on trust and freedom, a few details - together with a link to an article on each.

Covered in Case Studies

Buurtzorg	Belgian Ministry of Social Security	Haier
Happy		WL Gore
Cook	Toyota	Basecamp
	Google	Reddico

Covered in Self-Managing Organisations (previous chapter)

Mayden	Zappos	Github
Buurtzorg	Valve	Medium
Local Cornerstone	Basecamp	NW Care Co-operative
Reddico	Morning Star	Cocoon
U2i	WL Gore	Semco
	Treehouse	

Further Trust-based Organisations

37Signals	Black Lives Matter	Buffer
AES		Burning Man
Basecamp	Blinkist	Cougar

Crisp

Dreamhost

Elbdudler

Endenburg Elektrotechniek

Enspiral

Equinor

Evangelical School Berlin Centre

Everlane

EZBZ

Favi

Gini

Gumroad

Fitzii

Handelsbanken

Haufe-umantis

Heiligenfeld

Hengeler Mueller

Heman Miller

HolocracyOne

Incentro

Innocent

John Lewis

Kickstarter

Lumiar Schools

Menlo Innovation

Mondragon

Nearsoft

Netflix

NextJump

Nixon McInnes

Nucor

Orpheus Chamber Orchestra

Ozvision

Patagonia

Phelps Agency

Pixar

Premium-Cola

Promon Group

Propellernet

Red Hat

School in the cloud

Schuberg Philis

Social Interest Group

SocialAdventures

Spotify

stok

Sun Hydraulics

Timpsons

TLC

UKTV

Whole Foods

WP Haton

Zalando Technology

Zappos

Zingermans

Some of these are based on the list in Brave New Work by Aaron Dignan.

HCL: Employees first, customers second

At this 150,000 strong Indian IT outsourcing company, the focus is on supporting their people – so that they will deliver great service to customers. Interview with CEO Vineet Nayar:

http://bit.ly/EmpFirstCustSec

24. Case Study: Netflix

Book Review: No Rules Rules: Netflix and the Culture of Reinvention by Reed Hastings and Erin Meyer

Adequate performance gets a generous severance package

That is the controversial proposal that was originally shared in the Netflix Culture Deck. As Erin points out, this appears to violate the principles of "psychological safety", that if you want to encourage innovation you should develop an environment "where people feel safe to dream, to speak up and take risks".

Reed explains that this approach results from 2001, when Netflix had to make redundancies and kept those they saw as most talented: "we'd just let go of a third of the workforce, yet the office was suddenly buzzing with passion, energy, and ideas. Suddenly, we were doing far more work—with 30 percent fewer employees … We learned that a company with really dense talent is a company everyone wants to work for."

A team not a family

Since then Netflix has focused on building "talent density". Many companies describe themselves as like a family. Netflix does not. Their comparison is to a sports team where, if your performance drops, you could be on the way out.

Reed argues, "a team with one or two merely adequate performers brings down the performance of everyone on the team."

The Keeper Test

Every manager at Netflix is encouraged to consider, for each of their people: "If a person on your team were to quit tomorrow, would you try to change their mind?"

If the answer is No, then it's time to let them go. There is no four-month PIP (Performance improvement plan). They are paid off straight away.

In turn employees are encouraged to ask "The Keeper Test Prompt": "If I were thinking of leaving, how hard would you work to change my mind?", and - if you wouldn't work hard - what do i need to change?

Reed sees this as different from "rank-and-yank", used previously by Microsoft and General Electric to fire the 10% worst performers in any team.

Hire "rock stars"

Reed argues that, in creative jobs, the best performers are not just twice as good as the average ones but often 25 or 100 times better: "I could hire ten to twenty-five average engineers or I could hire one "rock-star" and pay significantly more than what I'd pay the others. We'd be relying on one tremendous person to do the work of many. But we'd pay tremendously."

A culture of freedom and responsibility

The other side of Netflix culture is a remarkable level of trust. Jennifer Nierva describes how at her previous job, at Hewlett-Packard, she had to get 20 levels of approval to employ consultants on a $200,000 contract. It took her six weeks and endless frustrating phone calls.

Joining Netflix she came up with a $1 million marketing proposal and asked her boss who she had to get to sign it off. "Nobody", was the answer. "Just sign it and send it back."

As Reed explains, "At most companies, the boss is there to approve or block the decisions of employees. This is a surefire way to limit innovation and slow down growth. When the boss steps out of the role of "decision approver," the entire business speeds up and innovation increases."

When Sheryl Sandberg, Chief Operating Officer at Facebook, spent a day shadowing Reed she commented: "The amazing thing was to sit with you all day long and see that you didn't make one decision!"

Lead with context, not control

Netflix is not of course a self-managing organisation. Instead of telling people what to do, though, managers are expected to set the context.

Adam Del Deo, head of Netflix's documentaries, was wondering whether to increase his $2.5 million bid for the documentary Icarus. He asked his boss, Ted Sarandos, if he should bid more.

Ted responded not with a decision but with context: "Is it THE ONE? Is it going to be a massive hit. If its THE ONE, get the movie."

As Reed continues, "When one of your people does something dumb, don't blame that person. Instead, ask yourself what context you failed to set. "

Farm for Dissent

But Netflix staff are not expected to make decisions on their own. Instead the approach is similar to the Advice Process: "We don't expect employees to get approval from their boss before they make decisions. But we do know that good decisions require a solid grasp of the context, feedback from people with different perspectives, and awareness of all the options."

If someone uses the freedom Netflix gives them to make important decisions without soliciting others' viewpoints, Netflix considers that a demonstration of poor judgment.

If you are a Netflix employee with a proposal, you create a shared memo explaining the idea and inviting dozens of your colleagues for input. They will then leave comments electronically in the margin of your document, which everyone can view.

"Farm for dissent. Socialize the idea. Test it out. This sounds a lot like consensus building, but it's not. With consensus building the group decides; at Netflix a person will reach out to relevant colleagues, but does not need to get anyone's agreement before moving forward. They are the Informed Captain"

Mistakes

While you may be fired if you are felt to be performing only adequately you won't get fired for getting something wrong. "At Netflix, we try to shine a bright light on every failed bet. We encourage employees to write open memos explaining candidly what happened, followed by a description of the lessons learned."

"Don't seek to please your boss. Seek to do what is best for the company"

"At most companies, even at those who have leaders who don't micromanage, employees seek to make the decision the boss is most likely to support."

There are lots of examples in the book of where Netflix staff do the opposite of what the boss would support. In one case senior director Ted Sarandos is discussing the release of The Blacklist Season 2 and a guy four levels down hierarchically from Ted "pipes up and tells him he was missing something and hadn't understood the licence deal." At the end of the session Ted thanks him for his contribution.

"We now say that it is disloyal to Netflix when you disagree with an idea and do not express that disagreement. By withholding your opinion, you are implicitly choosing to not help the company."

No Rules Rules

Netflix is famous for its vacation policy ("take some") and its expenses policy ("act in Netflix's best interest").

On the need for holidays, Reed gives the example of a guy who "often went to an isolated place. Each time he came back he had a fantastic new idea for how to move the business forward." However unlimited vacation depends crucially on the example from managers. While Reed takes six weeks off a year, Erin makes clear that some managers take less. In turn their staff feel unable to take advantage of the policy.

Interestingly the expenses policy was originally "spend money as if it were your own" but this didn't work for those who were profligate spenders in their personal life. Reed reckons the expenses policy probably results in 10% extra spending (due to business class travel on airlines) but is well worth it in terms of trust and speed: "Approval policies, decision making by committee, and contract sign-offs all put hurdles in front of your employees so that they can't move quickly."

This is in contrast to his previous company, Push Software. There they had all sorts of policies: "we had, without much thought, dummy-proofed the work environment. The result was that only dummies wanted to work there."

Total Transparency

At Happy we make all finances available to our staff, and teach them how to use them. However we are a private company. For a publicly traded company like Netflix there are strict rules on what can be shared. If anybody uses information to buy shares, knowing they are set to go up, it can be a criminal offence.

Indeed before they show the figures, they show this slide: "You go to jail if you trade on this …. Or if your friend does. Confidential. Do not share."

Pump up Candour

Netflix takes feedback seriously, at every level. Staff are expected to provide others with clear candour to help them improve.

Indeed it is so embedded that Erin describes how, as an outside speaker, she received clear feedback in the middle of her talk. Giving a presentation on international cultural differences, she was told her facilitating was undermining her message, as she always went to the first people to raise their hands - who were normally Americans. And it meant she was able to change her approach for the rest of the talk.

Initially there was an annual survey based on "Stop, Start, Continue" (what should this person stop doing, start doing, continue doing). However now the most common approach is to hire a private room in a restaurant for a team and, over the meal, get everybody to provide feedback to each of their colleagues.

A core principle here is: "Only say about someone what you will say to their face."

It sounds impressive. We all know we would like to improve but few companies provide true radical candour.

Erin reveals the figures from a survey: "57 percent of respondents claim they would prefer to receive corrective feedback to positive feedback. 72 percent felt their performance would improve if they received more corrective feedback. 92 percent agreed with the comment, "Negative feedback, if delivered appropriately, improves performance."

"With candour, high performers become outstanding performers."

"With candour, high performers become outstanding performers. Frequent candid feedback exponentially magnifies the speed and effectiveness of your team or workforce. Set the stage for candour by building feedback moments into your regular meetings. Coach your employees to give and receive feedback effectively. As the leader, solicit feedback frequently and respond with belonging cues when you receive it. Get rid of jerks as you instil a culture of candour."

Stop Being Busy

Among all this I love the fact that Reed is not one of those executives who works all hours and is endlessly busy. In February 2020, just before the pandemic, I wrote a LinkedIn post stating that, as a CEO, I was not busy. I argued that senior people "need to step out of the way, stop with the endless meetings and get a life."

However I am head of a 25 person company. Reed Hastings runs a $25 billion enterprise, employing ten thousand people. So I am delighted to find he agrees: Reed "believes so deeply in dispersed decision-making that, by his model, only a CEO who is not busy is really doing his job."

The results have been astounding. $10,000 invested in Netflix at its public offering in 2002 would be worth $3.5 million now. Netflix now has a higher revenue per employee even than Apple. And, according to a 2018 survey from Hired, Netflix rates no. 1 (above Apple and Google) as the place tech workers would most like to work for.

25. Bibliography & Sources of the Nickables

Many of the nickables come from Happy clients and have been selected from examples they have given from the ideas shared at our quarterly CEO breakfast and the monthly Happy Workplaces webinar. Other examples come from the speakers at our conferences.

Other sources include a range of books. I love books that tell stories and give real examples, real nickables. Books included are listed below.

Recommended on Creating Great Workplace Cultures

Happy Manifesto, Henry Stewart, 2013

The source of the ten principles included here, and also contains many more stories and examples for each of them.

Maverick, Ricardo Semler, 1993

A classic. Brazilian businessman Ricardo Semler explains how he inherited his father's manufacturing business and turned it from a company with no trust to one where workers had the freedom to set their own targets, organise their workplaces, choose their managers and even – in some cases – set their own salaries.

Reinventing Organisations, Frederick Laloux, 2014

Again, a classic. Sub-title: A Guide to Creating Organizations Inspired by the Next Stage of Human Consciousness. This hugely influential book explores "Teal" organisations, those based on self-managing.

Brave New Work, Aaron Dignan, 2019

Are you ready to reinvent your organisation. A key work on self-managing organisations.

Work Rules, Laszlo Bock, 2015

"Insights from inside Google that will transform how you live and work", by Google's Head of People. A great insight into the culture of Google and packed with evidence based approaches.

Team of Teams, General Stanley McChrystal, 2015

"The new rules of engagement for a complex world", McChristal uses lessons from his own experience in Iraq and other companies to promote more empowered ways of working.

Employees First, Customers Second, Vineet Nayar, 2010

Vineet, CEO of HCL Technologies (an Indian outsourcing company employing over 70,000 people), explains his focus: if you focus on your employees, they in turn will focus on the customers.

Becoming a Better Boss, Julian Birkinshaw, 2013

An employee's-eye view of what makes a great boss—and how you can become one, from LBS Professor – listed in the Thinkers50.

It doesn't have to be crazy at work, Jason Fried and David Heinemeier Hansson, 2018

The founders of software company Basecamp explain how they've created a company that avoids long hours and overwork, and instead encourages a life outside work.

Delivering Happiness, Tony Hsieh, 2010

The CEO of Zappos explains how he built a radically different company, renowned for its fabulous customer service, based on focusing on the happiness of his people.

Powerful, Patty McCord, 2018

McCord explains how, as Chief Talent Officer at Netflix, she helped create a high-performing culture based on freedom and responsibility.

Leading with Happiness, Alexander Kjerulf, 2017

"How the Best Leaders Put **Happiness** First to Create Phenomenal Business Results and a Better World" by Danish happiness guru Alexander Kjerulf.

Superengaged, Niki Gatenby, 2018

"How to transform business performance by putting people and purpose first"

How Google Works, Eric Schmidt & Jonathan Rosenberg, 2014

Ex-CEO Schmidt gives some great insights into the workings of the search giant.

Radical Candour, Kim Scott, 2017

As well promoting a kind of tough love, Kim gives great examples from her experience at Apple, Twitter and Google.

The Excellence Dividend, Tom Peters, 2018

"Meeting the Tech Tide with Work That Wows and Jobs That Last"

Multipliers, Liz Wiseman, 2017

The acclaimed *Wall Street Journal* bestseller that explores why some leaders drain capability and intelligence from their teams while others amplify it to produce better results

50+ Transformational practices in freedom at work, Worldblu, 2017

A playbook for building a world-class culture

The Age of Agile, Stephen Denning, 2018

How agile is moving beyond software and transforming organisations in the modern business world.

The Joy of Work, Bruce Daisley, 2019

Ex-VP of Twitter, Bruce gives 30 practical examples that could help you become happier at work.

It's the Manager, Jim Clifton, Jim Harper, 2019

Based on extensive surveys by Gallup, this gives detailed evidence on what works to create effective, productive organisations. The most important factor, as the title suggests, is the manager.

Leading with Happiness, Alex Kjerulf, 2018

Alex, based at WooHoo in Copenhagen, was the first person I know to call himself a Chief Happiness Officer. This is a great book about real examples of how to create happy workplaces. Lots of stories.

Rules, No Rules by Reed Hastings and Erin Meyer

Reed and Erin describe the culture of Netflix, one of trust and freedom, of critical feedback but also one where underperformance is met with a "generous severance package".

Humanocracy by Gary Hamel

Gary Hamel is one of the lead figures in promoting self-managing organisations. IN this book he describes how to replace bureaucracy with humanocracy.

Also quoted

Mindful Work: How Meditation is Changing Business from the Inside Out , David Gelles, 2015

New York Times business reporter David Gelles explains how mindful managers are using meditation, yoga and other mindfulness techniques to boost leadership,

Things a little bird told me, Biz Stone, 2014

The story of Twitter from one of its co-founders.

Becoming, Michelle Obama, 2018

Only mentioned here briefly but a powerful account from the ex-First Lady.

Whoever makes the most mistakes wins, Richard Farson with Ralph Keyes

The paradox of innovation: Argues that failure is a key factor in a path toward success.

Winners, Alistair Campbell, 2015

Campbell (aide to Tony Blair) examines how **winners** tick, considers how they build great teams, analyses how these people deal with unexpected setbacks and new challenges. One of the best insights into strategy that I know of.

26. Blogs and Podcasts

For the latest thinking we recommend:

My Happy blog: Check out my regular articles and posts on LinkedIn, and my blogs on the Happy web site:
https://bit.ly/HappyHenry

Corporate Rebels: Joost Minaar and Pim de Morree gave up their jobs to tour the world to find the most exciting workplaces on the planet, especially those featuring self-management. They write a must-read twice-weekly blog: https://corporate-rebels.com/

Lisa Gill, Reimaginaire: Lisa is at the forefront of self-managing organisations. Her blog is at https://medium.com/@reimaginaire and she has a monthly podcast at http://leadermorphosis.co/.

Alex Kjerulf: Writes a blog on happiness at work at
https://positivesharing.com/

Dan Pink: Sign up to Dan's fortnightly newsletter:
https://www.danpink.com/

Frederick Laloux: The author of Reinventing Organisations has a video series based on "pay-what-you-can":
https://bit.ly/ReinventXX

Gary Hamel: A very insightful contributor, seeking to "light the fire of management innovation":
http://www.garyhamel.com/blog

27. Appendix: 80 Ideas for Happy Workplaces

1.	Find a way to delight a customer every day – starting today
2.	Find a way to delight one of your people every day – starting today
3.	Stop to say hello to colleagues and get to know them better
4.	Find ways to make working together more fun and sociable
5.	Pre-approve: A new approach, a problem to solve – get an individual or group to find a solution and then implement it without checking back with you
6.	Step out of approval: And resist the temptation to "improve" your people's ideas
7.	Give people the freedom to choose their own paths to achieving results
8.	Ensure there are clear principles to work within
9.	Ensure there are clear objectives to work towards & people feel they own them and are fully accountable for them
10.	Once they have job ownership, hold people to account & be tough with underperformance
11.	Help your people set up regular feedback, from the customer
12.	Get managers to step out of the way
13.	Stop telling people what to do
14.	Pass the knowledge on to your people, so they don't need things approved
15.	Have your people write their own job descriptions
16.	Let people choose their own job title (or abolish job titles altogether)
17.	Encourage disobedience (as long as keep within company's principles)
18.	Give full power and responsibility to front-line staff to change anything that is wrong
19.	Let people spend 10% of their paid time doing something of their own initiative (Google: 20%)
20.	Take real responsibility in your job. Lead beyond your defined

	authority
21.	Peer appraisal: have every person appraised by their peers, their fellow workers. (You survive and prosper by what your colleagues think of you)
22.	Set rules for the 98% trying to do a good job, not the 2% who aren't
23.	Let people decide their own salaries (Semco)
24.	Let people choose which two colleagues should assess their salary (St Lukes)
25.	In every interaction with others, make it a goal to leave them feeling good
26.	Don't treat people as you would want to be treated, treat them as they would want to be treated (especially if you are a manager)
27.	Give your people £25 each (or even just £10) to make the office better in some way
28.	Allow everybody to spend £100 (or even £500), without needing approval, to make something better for a customer
29.	Spot somebody doing something well and tell them – every day
30.	Thank two people today
31.	Make it the key role for management to make people feel good about themselves
32.	Smile!
33.	Find opportunities to laugh together
34.	Surprise people with cakes or ice cream
35.	Make the focus of your managers to serve their people
36.	Redraw your organisation chart as an upside-down pyramid: Put the managers at the bottom and the front-line staff at the top
37.	Reward and promote as much on how supportive and helpful people are, as much on their ability in their core job
38.	Change your annual appraisals to regular one-to-ones and four monthly check-ins to
39.	Help your people find a real challenge, and support them to achieve it

40.	Create a quiet space, where an individual's presence is trusted, respected and allowed to just be for a while.
41.	Pause and look up and recognise the beauty around us
42.	Ask your people what would make them happier. Then enable it.
43.	Make a habit of noting good things that happen each day. Indeed try sharing and telling everyone about the good things that happen each day?
44.	Err on the side of sharing more information than people need
45.	Make all information in the organisation available for everybody to see (excepting only the really personal stuff)
46.	Especially make the finances open, and train people how to understand them
47.	Make salaries open and transparent too, so your people can see what everybody earns
48.	Forget the qualifications, check the ability instead
49.	Ban the use of non-specific qualifications in recruitment (eg, "must have a degree")
50.	Test their ability to do the job, not their ability to talk about doing the job
51.	Involve the people they will work with in the recruitment. Get buy-in before they start
52.	Especially for managers, have them principally chosen by the people they will manage Get them to spend a day in the office, and get the people they will work with to decide whether to appoint (Pret)
53.	Let your people leave well, help them find a new job and leave them feeling good
54.	Look for the potential in all your people, find the hidden gems
55.	Create environments where people can experiment, try new things and succeed or – safely – fail
56.	Ensure there is no blame for trying something new and messing up
57.	Make a point of warmly praising/celebrating when people own up to things that went wrong
58.	Hold a staff meeting where everybody declares a mistake

	they've made, especially you - to cheers from everybody else.
59.	Be prepared to say "I got it wrong. That was my fault"
60.	Ensure your organisation has a purpose beyond profit
61.	Create an environment where people feel really proud to work there.
62.	Discover, and regularly review, the skills and resources your organisation has, that could bring real benefit to others
63.	Check everything your organisation does, not just the 1% to charity, against the benchmark of whether it helps society
64.	Pay your suppliers early, especially the sole traders and small businesses
65.	Reduce your environmental impact, a little more each year
66.	Set an example of working to your hours, and taking time off
67.	Help your people work to their hours and avoid a long hours culture. Your customers want your people relaxed, well rested and nourished
68.	Equip and help people to work at home, if they want to
69.	Get great at helping people measure their productivity, so they are judged on what they produce not the time spent producing it
70.	Remember that people's best ideas rarely come at the office, help them have wide experiences
71.	Let your people work out the way of working that suits them, agreed with their colleagues
72.	Help your people find 'me' time in their life balance, to do what they really enjoy
73.	Give yourself 'me' time: what do you really enjoy doing?
74.	Have every manager appraised by the people they manage
75.	Help people who want to, to become great people managers. Help those who don't want to, to do what they are good at
76.	Find a way for some people to get promoted without having to manage people
77.	Encourage people to call meetings with managers when they want them, not the other way round
78.	Let people choose their managers
79.	Focus on developing your people's strengths, more than

	addressing weaknesses
80.	Get people to spend their time doing what they are good at